Village U
— in —
WARWICKSHIRE

Village Walks
— in —
WARWICKSHIRE

Richard Shurey

COUNTRYSIDE BOOKS
NEWBURY, BERKSHIRE

First published 1997
© Richard Shurey 1997

COUNTRYSIDE BOOKS
3 Catherine Road
Newbury, Berkshire

ISBN 1 85306 485 8

Designed by Graham Whiteman
Maps and photographs by the author

Front cover photo taken by Bill Meadows
shows the village of Aston Cantlow.

Produced through MRM Associates Ltd., Reading
Printed by J. W. Arrowsmith Ltd., Bristol

Contents

WALK

Publisher's Note

We hope that you obtain considerable enjoyment from this book; great care has been taken in its preparation. Although at the time of publication all routes followed public rights of way or permitted paths, diversion orders can be made and permissions withdrawn.

We cannot of course be held responsible for such diversion orders and any inaccuracies in the text which result from these or any other changes to the routes nor any damage which might result from walkers trespassing on private property. We are anxious though that all details covering the walks are kept up to date and would therefore welcome information from readers which would be relevant to future editions.

Introduction

The English village, although it remains as an essential part of the countryside, has witnessed many changes of purpose over 4,000 years. Prehistoric man lived in village-like settlements – but probably for collective security purposes. The Celts tended to gather on the open uplands because they did not possess the tools to clear the dense lowland forests. This all changed with the arrival of the Anglo-Saxons, the Jutes, the Danes and the Vikings; they had the axes and simple implements to clear woodlands and establish settlements.

They put their marks on the landscape, determining the extent of their farmland with strip farming and grazing land – marks that we can often see on these rambles with ridges and hollows in the now-enclosed fields. We can therefore appreciate that most of England's villages were of some antiquity even before the Normans arrived.

In days that now seem far off the village contained all the needs of its people. They grew much of their own food and purchased their wants in the village stores (in my village of 600 inhabitants, in living memory there were three competing bakers). The children had their local school; they entertained themselves in the village hall and there was the essential pub. Literally above all – often on the highest point to be nearest to heaven – was the church. It is invariably the oldest building in pre-18th century villages, having survived from the Middle Ages.

It was difficult for village people to travel far from their homes even if they wanted to; life was so much simpler – and perhaps happier and less stressful. Such is progress.

Sadly, many of what I would say are the essential ingredients of a village (the church, the village shop, the 'local', the school and the village hall) are now missing. There are very few villages today which still possess all these five features and even as I visited villages for this book schools and shops were under threat. Places abound with names like The Old Post Office, The Olde Shoppe and The Old Mill House which no longer serve the community but are private houses.

But let us not become melancholic; the English village is still a wonderful place to visit, full of interest and often full of beauty – and always surrounded by intriguing networks of footpaths which have grown up with it. In the days before the motor car these were the essential lines of communication linking communities, farms, places of worship, and workplaces. Today we use them as escape routes into the tranquil countryside.

I have chosen the 20 villages to give a good spread of walks throughout Warwickshire. I cannot therefore pretend that they are necessarily the 20 prettiest places in the county, each clustered around a traditional green! But the charm of a village does lie in its uniqueness and the way it dovetails into the landscape, often by using local materials whether Cotswold mellowed stone or solid oak from the old Forest of Arden for timber-framed cottages.

Each walk is circular and is illustrated by a sketch map, designed to guide you to the starting point and give a simple but accurate idea of the route to be taken. However, for those who like the benefit of detailed maps, the relevant Ordnance Survey sheet is very much recommended, especially for identifying the main features of views. There are several from which to choose, but I have given the relevant Landranger (1:50000) number in each case.

Enjoy your walking through the wonderful countryside of Shakespeare's 'leafy' Warwickshire!

Richard Shurey

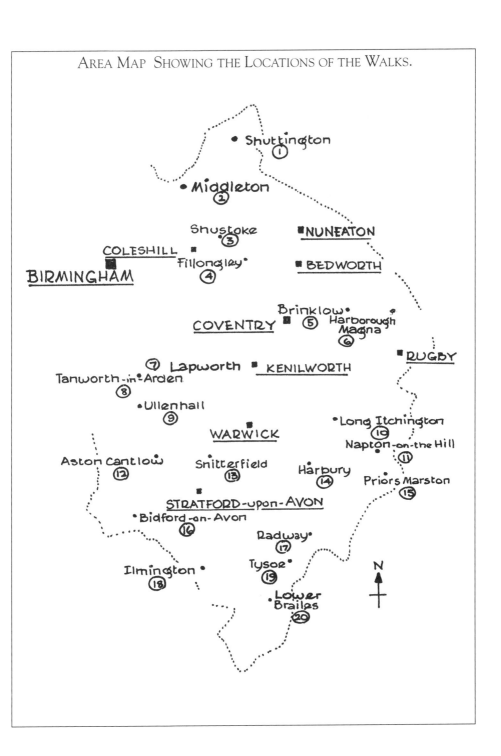

AREA MAP SHOWING THE LOCATIONS OF THE WALKS.

SHUTTINGTON

Length: 4 miles

Getting there: 3 miles from Tam-worth along the B5493 Ashby-de-la-Zouch road take the lane signed to the village.	Parking: Quiet roadsides. Maps: OS Landranger – Birmingham and surrounding	area (139) and Leicester and Coventry area (140). (GR 253053).

The view from this hilltop village was only made beautiful and spectacular in the mid-1930s, when the lush water meadows beside the fast flowing river Anker became flooded from the subsidence caused by Alvecote coal mines. These days there are willow-fringed pools (now the centre of a nature reserve) which attract a wide range of waterfowl and glint like sheets of silver in the rays of the western evening sun.

The monks of Alvecote Priory (founded by William Burdet in 1159) used to tramp over the same water meadows on their way to their chapel at Shuttington. The site of the chapel is now the parish church, although the only remaining Norman feature is the fine carved door-way, which some say was in fact removed formerly a mining community, like the hamlet of Alvecote. Along the canal, which is popular with holiday cruisers, we detour to the priory site – a pleasant spot for a picnic and a visit to the nearby nature reserve – before climbing the ridge back to Shuttington.

THE WALK

❶ Start by the green opposite Church Lane. Walk away from the road with the pub car park on your left. Pass houses (on left) and keep to the left of garages to a stile then climb another where three paths are signed.

❷ Take the middle path over a large meadow, making for a distant clump of willows. Go over a stile. Two paths are

from the priory. The church also has another distinction – east and west on the weathervane are placed the wrong way round so that the sun we mentioned earlier is the eastern evening sun in these parts!

On part of the route we walk along the towing path of the Coventry Canal. This 38-mile long waterway is in fact quite a rarity as it made a satisfactory profit for the shareholders right up to nationalisation. It was opened in 1790 and its main trade was to carry coal southwards from the Midland pits.

The walk starts with a pleasant path down from the hill and over meadows. It then nudges one of the pools before heading towards Amington Hall Farm. The Hall itself, seen in the distance, was once owned by the Abbey of Winchcombe – which probably explains why it was built in a Cotswold style. The farm borders the reeded river Anker, frequented by ducks. Over the water, the path goes to Amington, now a dormitory of Tamworth but

The ruins of Alvecote Priory.

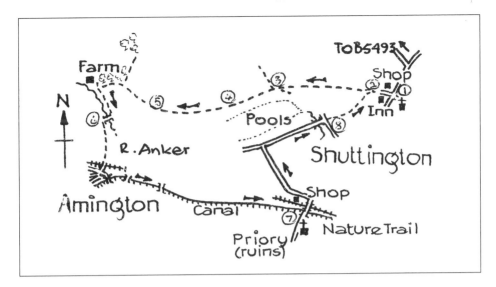

arrowed. Take the left-hand path to go over a stile to the right of a gate. Keep the direction to the far corner fence stile by a metal gate.

❸ On a tarmac vehicle way turn right a step or two. Ignore the metal gate (a bridleway) and keep ahead a yard or so to go over a step stile by a wooden gate. Continue by a left-hand wire fence to pass an electricity pylon. In a corner is a gateway and battery of stiles which you do not climb.

❹ Go through the gate and keep by the left-hand wire fence to a corner gate and fence stile. In the next meadow walk alongside a right-hand wire fence to a corner step stile. Maintain the heading in the next (often arable) field at the left-hand border.

❺ Go around a corner to pick up a bold tractor way alongside a left-hand hedge.

The tractor way goes through a gate and along a concrete farm 'road' to a junction of ways by the corner of a poplar wood. Turn left alongside the river and go over the footbridge.

❻ Take the arrowed direction over the pasture to a stile onto a vehicle way. Over the railway this becomes a road. At a junction bear left to the canal. On the towing path continue with the water on your right. Follow the canal to the road at bridge 59.

❼ Turn right on the road and cross the canal to visit the ruins of the priory. Retrace your steps over the canal then go over the railway. The lane goes through Alvecote to a T-junction. Turn right. Just across the narrow bridge over the river the road twists sharp right. Cross to the opposite path over a stile.

❽ Take the direction indicated to go over a meadow and cross a footbridge. Climb the hill, aiming to the left of houses, to a stile which we climbed on the outward route. Retrace your steps into Shuttington.

The church at Shuttington, with its fine Norman doorway.

MIDDLETON

Length: 3 miles

Getting there: 3 miles north-east of Sutton Coldfield along the A453 is a large roundabout. Take the A446. Within ¼ mile	take the lane on the left to Middleton. Parking: Quiet roadsides.	Map: OS Landranger – Birmingham and surrounding area (139). (GR 176983).

Middleton is in a quiet backwater and the countryside is a little oasis surrounded by several busy highways. There are many Middletons in England and this one is probably named because it is midway between two large towns (Sutton Coldfield and Tamworth). It was noted in the Domesday survey of 1086 and in White's 1850 *Directory* it was said to be an 'exten-

sive and well-built village'. It is, of course, still well-built but its size would now be described as modest and friendly.

These were the lands of the Willoughbys whose seat was the once splendid mansion of Middleton Hall. Sadly the house was abandoned to the elements for many years, then valuable sand and gravel was extracted from the grounds and all looked

---

FOOD and DRINK

The Green Man, once a farm on the Willoughby estate, is a very fine inn which is enlightened enough to open all day. I liked the Stuffed Yorkshire Pudding – a giant 'pud' with sausages and onion gravy served with Cheddar mash and vegetables – and vegetarians could choose the intriguing Red Dragon Bake. A coffee house serving a good range of refreshments is situated in the old stable block at Middleton Hall as part of the craft centre. This is open all year from Wednesday to Sunday (11 am to 5 pm). Refreshments are also available at the Hall when it is open on Sundays (2 pm to 5.30 pm) from Easter to October. The village shop is well stocked with picnic fare for your walk.

---

hopeless. However, enlightened, visionary folk are diligently restoring the Hall for the benefit of the public as a cultural and conservation centre. The situation is so very appropriate as in the 17th century it was the home of two great naturalists. Francis Willoughby (a founder member of the Royal Society) had a great interest in natural history and he was encouraged by John Ray, one of Britain's greatest naturalists who did much work on the classification of flora and fauna. There is a monument to Francis Willoughby (and other members of the family) in Middleton's church of John the Baptist. The site goes back to Anglo-Saxon times but the earliest masonry seen today is Norman

The old village pump in Middleton.

from the 12th century. There is a wonderful huge gilt clock on the 15th-century Perpendicular tower and just outside the churchyard is the ancient village pump. There was once a second inn in the village. A vicar of a few decades ago recorded in his fascinating diary that up to 1814 the parsonage was a pub.

A visit to Middleton Hall is a must on this walk. We follow the right of way along the drive which borders a lovely lake where swans glide through the water lilies. The return to Middleton is mainly across arable lands over clear paths.

THE WALK

❶ From the church follow the lane past the shop through the village to the A4091. Cross to the drive of Middleton Hall and walk along it to the entrance gates to the Hall by the moat.

❷ Do not go through the gates but swing left on the vehicle way to pass a little bungalow. By a junction of vehicle ways turn right so the car park and stable block (craft centre) are now on your right side.

❸ Follow the vehicle way past piles of sand and gravel and the buildings which were once a farm (when there was land to

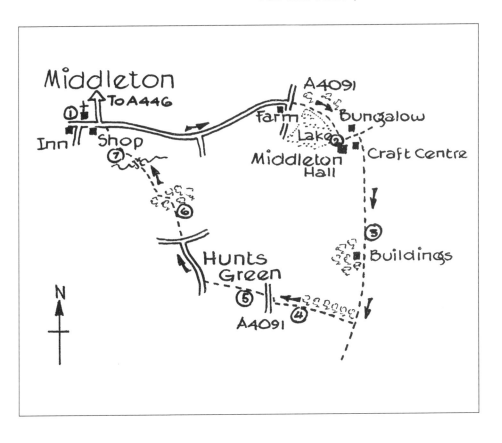

PLACES of INTEREST

Kingsbury Water Park is only a few miles southeast of Middleton. Until quite recently this was a derelict area of worked-out sand and gravel pits. Now many folk come here either for the watersports on the many pools or to see the great variety of water-fowl which frequent the region. There are adventure playgrounds, picnic areas and a very imaginative information centre. Refreshments are available. **Drayton Manor Park** is 2 miles north of Middleton. The house, once the home of Sir Robert Peel, the great statesman, was pulled down many years ago but now the grounds are unashamedly given over to fun. Among the well-kept gardens are fairground attractions, a zoo, boating lakes and so on. There are many refreshment places.

farm!) About ⅓ mile beyond the buildings turn right by an avenue of poplar trees. Over the stile walk between the trees along a clear (but slightly overgrown) path.

❹ Emerging from the trees in an arable field continue alongside the left-hand hedge. Go around the far corner to a stile to the main road. Cross, then turn right a few steps to a stile by an electricity sub-station. Cross directly over the field.

❺ Climb a stile then at once another. Keep ahead around a bank and pool to a stile to a lane. Turn right to a road junction. Cross to the signed path opposite. Keep to the right of a hedge and a garden then continue to a wood.

❻ Go left; the path is clear through the trees. At a division of ways after 100 yards bear right. Through a gap, leave the wood and follow the left-hand border of an arable field to a bridge over a brook. Keep ahead over a paddock field to a step stile.

❼ Take the arrowed direction across a rough pasture to a corner stile. Go along a fenced way then at the side of lawns to a gate to a road at Middleton. Turn left to the centre of the village.

SHUSTOKE

Length: 7½ miles

Getting there: Shustoke is 2½ miles east of Coleshill, on the B4114.

Parking: In the layby by the Plough inn.

Map: OS Landranger – Birmingham and surrounding area (139). (GR 228909).

Shustoke is a village of two halves; Shustoke proper has a pleasant mix of new and old properties but a mile distant is Church End, the ancient core, with the place of worship (on a Saxon site) built on a gentle hill 600 years ago. At the time of the Great Plague in 1650 the anxious villagers decided to leave their homes to establish the new village in the valley.

Gathered around the weathered red sandstone church, some of which dates from the last century when lightning destroyed much of the old structure, are old farmsteads, timber-framed barns, the rectory, dovecote, and school building. What was not destroyed by the lightning strike in 1886 was the monument to Sir William Dugdale (1605–86) the celebrated Warwickshire historian. He was born at the Old Rectory and lived for much of his life a mile or so away at the 17th-century mansion of Blyth Hall.

The name of Shustoke is also synonymous with the mile-long reservoirs which give Coventry and Nuneaton their water supply. They now also provide water for a sailing club and anglers.

Two long distance paths meet at Shustoke and the walk includes lengths of both of them. The Heart of England Way follows a snake-like route through the beautiful countryside from Cannock Chase to Bourton-on-the-Water. The Centenary Way which runs from Kingsbury Water Park to Quinton marked the 100 years of local government in Warwickshire.

This walk starts from the little green in Shustoke (Scotescote in the Domesday survey); here there is a board which displays several rambles along footpaths around the village. Next to the inn is the village pound where stray animals were penned. We walk along the vehicle way beside the reservoir then cross the river Bourne to the hamlet of Botts Green.

From here for the next mile or so there are delightful typically English country lanes – narrow and hedged and giving constantly changing views. Foul End is a misnomer as it is deep into a fine, lonely countryside. The return to Shustoke is along the Heart of England Way then again beside the fir-bordered reservoir.

THE WALK

❶ Opposite the inn, start down a vehicle way. There is soon a view over the reservoir. Leaving the vehicle way follow the footpath arrows and Centenary Way emblems to arable lands. Keep ahead to pass a signed junction of paths and at the border of an often arable field with woods on the left.

❷ At a junction of paths turn left over a stile. Follow the path to soon border a brook on the right. Go over a substantial bridge to reach a railway. Cross the tracks through gates and walk along a wide track to a road. Turn right. Pass a junction. A few steps further take a path up the bank, left.

❸ Go over a metal fence stile to an arable field. Strike out over the open field to pick up a left-hand hedge to a far corner stile.

PLACES of INTEREST

Maxstoke Priory ruins are along lanes 3 miles south of Shustoke. The priory was founded in 1336 for Augustinian canons. The inner gatehouse has been converted into a farmhouse and the ruins merge with farmyard buildings. A mile or so away is **Maxstoke Castle** where Richard III stayed before the battle of Bosworth.

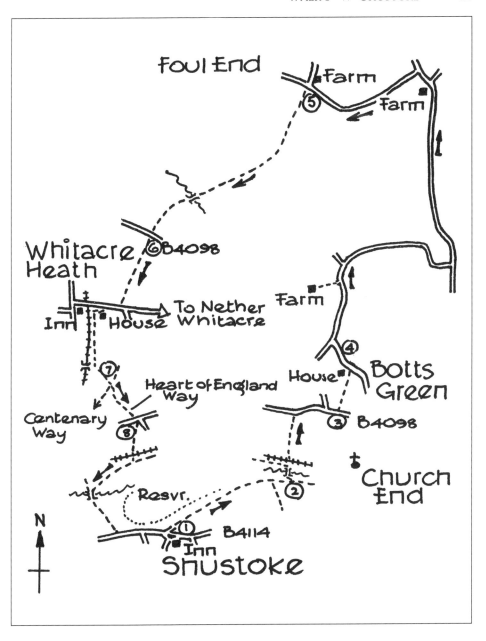

Maintain the direction over a pasture to pass through a metal gate. Along a house drive is a lane. Turn left.

❹ At a junction go right. Pass a farm 'road' to another junction. Keep ahead (signed 'Hurley'). At the next junction

Church End, the old centre of the village.

(no sign) turn left. By a farm the road divides; bear left. Within a few steps take the unsigned lane left. By New House Farm the lane splits. Take the signed bridleway along the wide farm track, left. Here we join the Heart of England Way.

❺ Follow the track to a field and continue on the well-used bridleway over the open field to pass through a gate in the very far right-hand corner. Join a track and continue to a road. Cross over.

❻ Climb a stile to a pasture. Walk the length to a stile. Bear slightly left to climb a stile near a far corner. Turn left to a stile to a road. Turn right. Just before a railway bridge bear left to pass a house. (The pub is over the railway bridge.) Climb a stile, left, and follow the way near the railway on the right. At a footbridge bear left over the open field.

❼ At a stile is a junction of paths. Take the right-hand way (Centenary Way). Follow the track around the field to climb a stile. Take the path over the open field to a stile to a lane. Cross to the signed path opposite.

❽ Follow the left-hand border of an arable field for a few steps then strike out over the open field, aiming to the left of a wood. Go past a marker post and walk around the field to a railway crossing place over which you reach a junction of paths. Turn right to a field. Follow the border to a bridge. Turn left over the water. There is now a clear path to the main road. Turn left to Shustoke.

WALK 4

FILLONGLEY

Length: 4 miles

Getting there: 12 miles from Birmingham on the A45 take the B4102 to Meriden then Fillongley.	Parking: In quiet roads near the church.	Map: OS Landranger – Leicester and Coventry area (140). (GR 281871).

Fillongley is one of those old settlements that might have become a large town but through a quirk of history preferred to remain a small village, these days of (I would estimate) some 600 residents. That it was important can be gauged from the fact that it was granted the coveted right to hold a weekly market (on Mondays) and an annual fair. The winding brooks around Fillongley could also supply the water for the moats of not one but two castles. One was owned by the de Hastings family and the other was built by John de Segrave who was responsible for the execution of the Scottish hero William Wallace in 1305. Both castles survived until Oliver Cromwell reckoned they were a threat and had them demolished. Today they are only marked by the name of Castle Farm and the outlines of the moats.

The area around Fillongley is the countryside of George Eliot; it was here,

that she found inspiration to write such descriptive prose describing the landscape of 'dewy brambles and rank, tufted grass'. She was born on the Arbury estate a few miles north-east of the village, where her father was the land agent.

Fillongley is clustered around its Norman church which is noted for the colourful medieval glass in the windows. The font is Norman but it was rescued from use in a garden some years ago. There are still shops in Fillongley although the old trades have all but gone – the weavers such as George Eliot's Silas Marner are only recalled by the name of the Weaver's Arms inn, on the road to Astley.

The start of the walk is by the church. We go by the churchyard which has an ancient cross and the tomb of Isaac Pearson, uncle of George Eliot. Further on is a rather unusual house which was converted from a church; the work received a Civic Trust award in 1984. Footpaths cross arable and pastoral lands to pass the old timbered and red brick Red Hill Farm. The route goes to Corley Ash; the Jacobean Corley Hall, to the south-east, was said to have been the model for Hall Farm in *Adam Bede*. The return is over fields and past the embankments and hollows marking the site of one of Fillongley's castles.

THE WALK

❶ Take the lane by the church with the

FOOD and DRINK

For a picnic meal there are two stores for supplies, one with extended opening. In addition there are four inns in Fillongley and one about halfway along the route at Corley Ash. All are welcoming to walkers and all offer good, wholesome fare, the Manor House standing conveniently by the finishing place of the walk opposite the church. The inn at Corley Ash is the Saracen's Head with a determined looking Saracen on the sign! The salads here are particularly noteworthy and the ploughman's is excellent value.

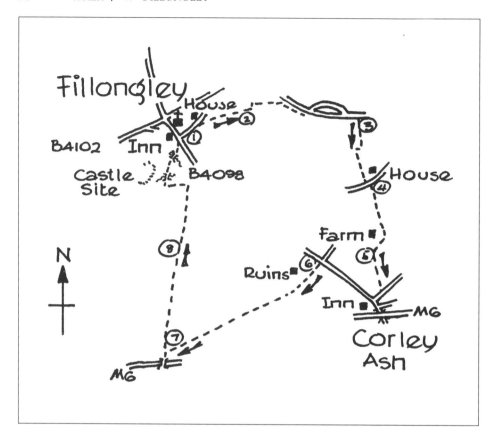

churchyard on your left. After 300 yards and opposite Church House paths are signed on the right into a recreation ground. Take the left-hand way along a paved path to a stile in a distant corner.

❷ Keep the heading over the open field. By a little pool turn left a step or two then resume the old direction which is signed by a tall wooden fence. Follow the path through rough scrubland to a road. Turn right. Within 250 yards take a signed path over a stile on the right.

❸ In the field walk by the right-hand border. In a corner take a path over a stile, right. Within a step or two regain the old direction over a stile by a metal gate. Continue up the pasture alongside the right-hand hedge to a stile. In the next field bear right to a stile onto a road.

❹ Go left then at once right; the path is signed and you follow the arrowed direction to climb a far corner stile. Go around the border of the next field to regain the old heading with Red Hill Farm away to the right. Staying by right-hand hedges follow the edge of the field around corners to reach a stile.

❺ Cross a meadow to a rough stile to the right of an off-white house. Continue to a road and turn right. At a road junction turn right. Within ⅓ mile there is another road junction. Turn left. The unsigned path is through a gate.

❻ In the pasture bear slightly left to a fence stile in the opposite hedge. There is a ruined building away to the right. The heading is now constant through fields with gates and fence stiles to show the way. Gradually we are nearing the motorway.

❼ A tall kissing-gate is reached. Immediately before it turn right. (On my survey a slight detour had to be made because of pipework in progress.) Walk alongside a left-hand hedge to a distant fence stile now seen. Go over a brook and continue by a right-hand hedge. By a pool keep the old heading over an open field.

PLACES of INTEREST

For the admirers of George Eliot there are many reminders of the great writer in the area. For example she was baptised in Chilvers Coton Church near Nuneaton. (She used the village as her 'Shepperton' in *Scenes of Country Life* – Nuneaton was 'Milby'.) **Arbury Hall** (the author's 'Cheverel Manor') is a wonderful example of 18th-century Gothic revival and open to the public, although South Farm, where George Eliot was born, cannot be visited. Her parents are buried at Chilvers Coton, and so on. Much about George Eliot can be gleaned at **Nuneaton** as the town is rightly proud to have the associations.

---

❽ Climb (or go under!) an awkward fence stile and keep ahead through a hedge gap to cross a brook. Again there is a right-hand hedge. In a corner turn left along the edge of the field to a stile to the old castle site. Bear right to cross a brook and corner stile and follow the clear path back to Fillongley.

BRINKLOW

Length: 5½ miles

Getting there: Brinklow is 4 miles along the B4027 from its junction with the A4082, 4 miles east of Coventry.	Parking: Park at side of Broad Street (the wide main street of the village.)	Map: OS Landranger – Leicester and Coventry area (140). (GR 436796).

Brinklow is a very ancient village as is evidenced by the 'tump' which was a burial ground in pre-Roman times. The Romans took their Fosse Way around it and utilised the strategic upland. At the time of King Stephen the Mowbrays built a motte and bailey castle and it is said to be one of the finest such sites in the country.

Today Brinklow has the air of a small town, with an almost continuous frontage along the main street. There is still a good assortment of shops and a nice amalgam of different building styles including cottages capped by thatch and timber-framed houses. In past days it was the centre of candlemaking, basket-weaving and silk industries.

WALK 5 ✳ BRINKLOW   29

❶ Walk along Broad Street to pass the church, built in the Perpendicular style but with quite a lot of 13th-century work. There are several very colourful windows. Nearby you will see The Crescent, a most attractive row of cottages where flowers tumble from the window boxes in summertime. Out of the village go along Lutterworth Road. Immediately over a bridge across a brook (300 yards past a speed derestriction sign) take a signed path to the left.

❷ In the pasture follow the edge of the brook (on the left) then bear right to go into the next field. About two-thirds of the way along the right-hand boundary climb a fence stile and cross a plank bridge. Walk directly across the field, aiming towards an electricity pole which carries a grey transformer. Go through the nearby gate to a lane.

FOOD and DRINK

Brinklow has a splendid selection of inns to suit all tastes. The Raven serves standard fare excellently. There are special rates for senior citizens and vegetarian meals are also available. Not far away is the White Lion. This freehouse gives a good welcome to a hungry walker. In addition the village has a fish and chip shop and a Chinese take-away. The shops sell a wide range of food and drink if you wish to make up a picnic. In Stretton under Fosse, on the route, the village store has long closed but the hamlet still has its pub. The Union Jack Inn is proudly patriotic with a splendid British Bulldog on the sign.

The village was noted for its alehouses in the last century when the nearby Oxford Canal brought much trade and prosperity. Even today I counted four inns – and there may have been more tucked away in the back streets!

The walk starts at the church of St John the Baptist on a lofty site. It continues over sheep pastures and under the canal to reach Stretton Wharf, once a busy depot at the end of a branch of the waterway. These days it is an industrial estate and the still waters are only disturbed by ducks and moorhens. Over lonely countryside the route comes to the hamlet of Stretton under Fosse where the premises of the old smithy are now used for selling antiques, then nudges the extensive grounds of Newbold Revel, the seat of Sir Thomas Malory from 1433 and where he wrote his epic *Morte d'Arthur*. Beyond another fine mansion (the intriguingly-named Town Thorns), we return to Brinklow by walking along the earthworks of the motte and bailey castle.

PLACES of INTEREST

West of Brinklow towards Coventry is **Coombe Country Park**, a wonderful area centred on Coombe Abbey. This was the home of Cistercian monks from 1150 until the Dissolution of the Monasteries when it passed to John Dudley, the Duke of Northumberland. It is now owned by the City of Coventry and is fine for walks and picnics. **Coventry** itself has a splendid cathedral which is alongside the remains of the bombed out shell of the old cathedral church of St Michael. There is plenty of parking and the pedestrian ways make shopping pleasant in the city.

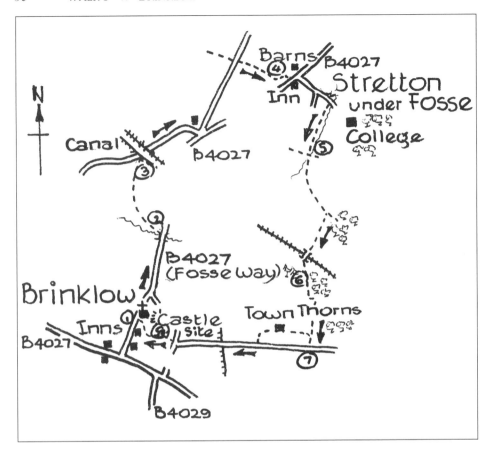

❸ Turn right. Go under the tunnels carrying the canal and the busy main line railway. Keep ahead to a road junction. Take the lane to the left by The Wharf. Within ½ mile and opposite a parking layby take an unsigned path on the right. Walk alongside the hedge. About two-thirds of the way along the hedge climb a double step stile beside a gate.

❹ In a bumpy pasture the next stile is by a metal gate and tucked in a corner well to the right of two Dutch barns. Continue to a lane at Stretton under Fosse. Turn left, then right along a narrow lane by the pub. When the lane divides continue left along the private drive (a public bridleway). Turn right by the white gates to Newbold Revel house. The grand mansion we see today (now a Prison Service Training Centre) was built in 1716 for Sir Fulwar Skipwith.

❺ The bridleway soon continues over a vehicle drive. Keep ahead on the tractor way. Before a wood take a footpath off the main track to the right. The farm way goes to a gate to arable lands. Walk over the open field to a bridge over the railway. Bear left to continue to the left of a clump of fir trees to the corner of a wood.

❻ Follow the path at the side of the wood, keeping the trees on your left. At the end of the wood go left then at once right to regain the old heading. Keep at the right-hand border of a field. Walk ahead through gates to join a vehicle drive to a lane.

❼ Turn right. The entrance to Town Thorns is passed and the canal is crossed to reach a road junction. Keep the old direction to climb a stile to a pasture and then take the arrowed route.

❽ Walk over a ridge and furrow field to a stile. To the right is the grassy 'tump'. Follow the arrowed path left to walk above the ditches of the old castle. We reach a meeting of signed paths and two stiles. Turn left to drop down to Broad Street at Brinklow.

Brinklow.

HARBOROUGH MAGNA

Length: 2½ miles

Getting there: Harborough Magna is on the B4112, 3 miles north of Rugby.	Parking: There is limited road-side parking near the church.	Map: OS Landranger – Leicester and Coventry area (140). (GR 477793).

At the Domesday survey of 1086 Harborough was recorded as Herdeberge and probably derived its name from 'the hill of the herd'. The survey revealed that it had a mill and its own priest. Its growth has been slow and even today there are only about 350 inhabitants.

This was once a very self-contained community with its own shops, wheelwright and the all important blacksmith; folk worked locally on the farms, in the timber yards on the banks of the Oxford Canal or on the large estates. Nowadays Rugby provides most of the employment with few workers required on the land. There is still a popular inn, but the humble little school which was built with such enthusiasm in 1845 has closed and the children are bussed elsewhere.

The church is dedicated to All Saints;

There was a major restoration in the last century but it was perhaps a little over zealous. The fine clock was installed ten years ago and shows the signs of the four Evangelists.

The walk starts from the church then goes over pastures and along winding lanes to the Oxford Canal. The route continues along the towing path and over a fine wrought iron bridge where a now-defunct branch canal was cut. The final leg is through woodlands then along the bridleway, back to the village.

its tower was built in Perpendicular style in Victorian times but parts of its stonework go back to the 13th century.

THE WALK

❶ From the church walk down Church

The now redundant village school in Harborough Magna.

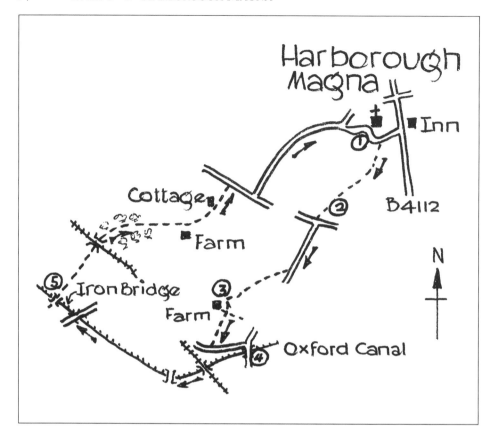

Hill. Within 150 yards and by a '40' speed sign take a signed path over a stile to the right. In the pasture follow the arrowed direction to another stile. Walk over a ridge and furrow pasture to the far right-hand corner.

❷ Climb a stile and follow the clear path through a copse to a lane by a junction. Cross to the opposite lane. Within 350 yards look for an unsigned path on the right over a fence stile. (A step stile and sign may be in place soon!). Aim to the right of the farmhouse to climb a stile in the wire fence.

❸ Continue along a way in front of the farmhouse to cross the drive over stiles. In a sheep pasture walk the length to the far right-hand corner. Climb a stile to a lane. Turn left to a road junction. Turn right to

---

PLACES of INTEREST

Rugby is only a few miles from Harborough Magna and has much of interest. At 5 Hillmorton Road the poet Rupert Brooke was born. The celebrated public school is in the centre of the town and has many attractive buildings. There is a statue to Thomas Hughes, the author of *Tom Brown's Schooldays.*

cross the canal. This waterway was built to the design of James Brindley but he was to die when only 16 of the 77 miles were completed. It was finally finished in 1790. To keep down the number of locks it followed twisting contours which greatly added to its length but it still suffers from a shortage of water during dry spells.

❹ At once turn right to gain the towing path. Follow the waterway and eventually go over the wrought iron bridge by the old branch canal. At bridge number 38 leave the canal. Climb the bank, left, to a bridleway. Turn right to cross the water.

❺ Follow the track under the railway and through a wood to soon pass a farmhouse. Continue along the drive to pass Lilac Cottage. Such a pretty garden – but the little windows should peep underneath a roof of thatch! At a road go right then take a lane left signed to Harborough Magna.

The fine wrought iron bridge over the Oxford Canal.

LAPWORTH

Length: 4½ miles

Getting there: 10 miles south of Birmingham on the A3400 Stratford road, take the B4439 eastwards. Within 1½ miles turn right along a lane to Lapworth church.	Parking: Limited parking is available by the church.	Map: OS Landranger – Birmingham and surrounding area (139). (GR 164712).

Lapworth is a village scattered over a large area (because isolated settlements were established in the many clearings in the Forest of Arden). The church, for example, is a couple of miles from the village store, post office and railway station. It is a popular area for commuters and there are many fine houses.

St Mary's church is on a gentle, wooded hill where there has been a place of worship for 800 years. There is much evidence of the Norman builders and the lovely spire is almost detached from the nave (perhaps because there was no room elsewhere with the lane running so close).

FOOD and DRINK

The Punch Bowl, is actually on the route, east of Packwood House, and is a splendid new pub built in an old style with dormers and attractive brick-work, replacing a humble farmworkers' hostelry which was destroyed by fire. There is always a wide range of dishes (including suggestions for vegetarians and children) on the menu; many are unusual but the old favourites like steak and kidney pies and 'naughty but nice' puddings are very popular. Look out too for the wonderful value meals such as the 'two for the price of one'. Another convenient inn (on the opposite bank of the canal to our towing path) is the Boot with a good range of standard fare and 'specials'. The village store at Lapworth will provide provisions for a picnic.

Lapworth's heyday was during the Canal Age with two great waterways meeting in the parish and inns where the bargees were offered refreshments. The nearby section of the Grand Union Canal (then the Birmingham and Warwick) dates from 1842 and it nudges the older Stratford-upon-Avon Canal which was fully opened in 1816.

The walk starts over undulating coun-tryside where backward glances give wonderful views of the hilltop church. Field paths out of the vale lead to Drawbridge Farm, whose name derives from the unusual bridge, close by, which has to be raised to allow the canal craft to proceed. Over mead-ows there is a delightful vista of Packwood House. The route takes you over lawns which are a yellow sea of daffodils in spring-time, then through sheeplands along a fine avenue of chestnut trees. The return is on the towing path of the Stratford-upon-Avon Canal, a haven for wildfowl, and beside the numerous locks of Lapworth Flight.

THE WALK

❶ Opposite the gate to the church climb a stile to a pasture. Walk by a left-hand barn and drop down to pass through a gate. Keep the heading over the brow of the hill then drop down to a stile and plank bridge over a brook.

❷ Turn right in a field showing ridges and hollows of strip farming. Climb a corner fence stile by the hidden brook. Keep ahead by the right-hand border of a large meadow. Climb a stile under an oak tree.

❸ Maintain the same general heading over the crown of the small hill ahead. Go through a metal gate and take the arrowed direction alongside a right-hand hedge and then a wire fence. Climb a stile by a

PLACES of INTEREST

Packwood House and gardens (National Trust) are open from April to the end of September (Wednesday to Sunday). The timber-framed house contains a wealth of furniture and tapestries. **Baddesley Clinton** (National Trust) is 3 miles east of Lapworth church. It is a moated manor house dating from the 14th century with (especially for the young at heart) ingeniously concealed priest holes to discover. The building has been little altered since 1634. Open from March to the end of September (Wednesday to Sunday). Licensed restaurant. **Temple Balsall** is 6 miles along lanes north-east of Lapworth. This was the base of the Knights Templars who protected the route for pilgrims to the Holy Land in the 12th century. We can see the chapel (much restored) and the refectory. Nearby is the Hospital – 17th-century almshouses founded by Lady Katherine Leveson who was the grand-daughter of Robert Dudley, Queen Elizabeth's favourite.

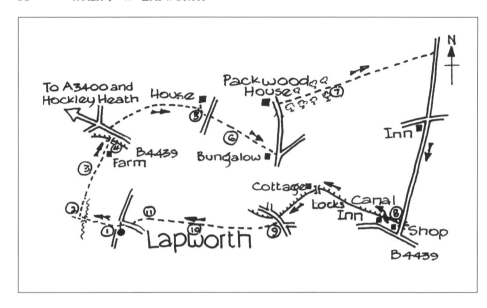

gate between the barns and house of a farmstead.

❹ Walk along the drive and over the drawbridge canal bridge to a road. Cross and turn left. Within a few yards turn right over a stile and along a signed path. Walk the length of an elongated meadow to pass through a far hedge gap. In the next field continue near the right-hand border to climb a corner stile.

❺ Continue a few steps at the side of an arable field then go through a hedge gap left to a house drive. Turn right to a lane. Cross to the opposite step stile to parkland. Take the arrowed heading to pass a waymark post.

❻ Keep ahead to a stile to an arable field. Turn left and walk around the edge and corner to a rather hidden stile. Go through a rough pasture then over another stile.

Continue at the border of a meadow and garden (bungalow on the right) to a road. Turn left and keep ahead at the junction. Packwood House, which you come to on the left, dates from Tudor times. The splendid 113-acre garden is unique, with its 17th-century Yew Garden representing the Sermon on the Mount. In the garden wall are 'bee-boles' – niches in which straw beehives are kept. Take the footpath opposite the house – up steps and through a metal gate.

❼ Walk along an avenue of chestnut trees and maintain the heading to a lane. Turn right. Go straight over at the crossroads (the Punch Bowl is on the right). Follow the lane to cross the canal bridge (the shop is nearby). At once over the water turn right to the towing path. Many species of duck, moorhens, Canadian geese and swans may be seen along this stretch.

Delightful Packwood Hall.

❽ Follow the towing path (with the water on your right side) then cross the canal and continue with the water now on the left. Go up the Lapworth Flight. By a cottage the towing path again changes sides. At the next road bridge leave the waterway. By the road climb a stile to a meadow.

❾ Walk by the left-hand hedge. Go through a far corner gap and maintain the direction still by a left-hand border to climb the rise to a far corner kissing-gate into a cricket field. Follow the arrowed way to a step stile to the right of the score-board.

❿ In a meadow keep the old heading to a corner stile. Two paths are signed here. Keep ahead to walk by a pool in a deep hollow (on the left) to a far stile. Continue by another pool then at the bottom of a lawn of a mansion climb a stile to a pasture.

⓫ Go alongside the right-hand border to a stile to Tapster Lane. This no through road used to be a tranquil route to the beautiful Tapster valley but, despite many protests from environmental groups, the M40 was eventually sited there. Turn right to return to the church.

TANWORTH-IN-ARDEN

Length: 3½ miles

Getting there: From Hockley Heath (10 miles south of Birmingham on the A3400) take the B4101 westwards. Within 3 miles turn left along the lane to Tanworth-in-Arden.	Parking: Quiet roadsides around the green.	Map: OS Landranger – Birmingham and surrounding area (139). (GR 113705).

Tanworth-in-Arden was once a clearing in the Forest of Arden – the Anglo-Saxon Tanworth or 'Thane's worth'. There used to be much confusion with Tamworth and 'in Arden' was added to the name earlier this century. Many manors were located within the extensive parish, including Umberslade, Codbarrow, Clayhall, Sidenhall, Beetlesworth, Lodbroke, Cheswicke and Crewenhale, and on large scale maps of the area their sites can be seen as moats. The families of the de Mowbrays, de Montforts, Beauchamps and Archers are interwoven in the intricate patterns of ownership.

THE WALK

❶ From the village green go down Well Lane. Within a step or two go through a kissing-gate to the churchyard. Follow the stone path through the churchyard (with the church on the left side) to a gate to a hill pasture. Walk down the hill alongside a left-hand fence to a gate onto a lane.

❷ Turn right. Within 40 yards take a signed path, left. Continue alongside a garden and climb a stile to a meadow. Keep ahead to climb a step stile, right. Regain the old heading now by a left-hand hedge. Over a stile in a corner turn right. Follow two sides of an arable field.

❸ In a far corner where the field is 'squeezed' go over a wooden-railed footbridge. Cross a small field then go under the railway. The Umberslade Children's Farm, the former Leasowe's Farm, is to the left. Swing right around a wood to a stile into a large pasture. Follow the arrowed direction to continue over the open field, passing two isolated oak trees.

FOOD and DRINK

The Bell Inn, Tanworth is at the beginning – and end – of the route. This is an old-fashioned hostelry serving good food, such as fisherman's pie, chicken Kiev and an excellent cottage pie, and a fine selection of beers. Sitting under that spreading chestnut tree on a sunny day is also recommended. The village store is nearby and they sell a good selection of drinks and snacks.

This is a charming, 'so typical' English village. Here is the little green complete with the traditional spreading chestnut tree and the flower-bedecked pub, and surrounded by a lovely assortment of timber-framed and Georgian houses. Nearby are the former trademen's and professional men's cottages so we find the Butts, Old Boot Shop, the Doctor's House and the Bankhouse, all delightful residential properties these days. The peace of the village is maintained by being away from main roads. When the GWR railway came in 1908 it was routed discreetly to avoid the place.

The walk starts from the church – on a gentle hillside, the spire is a landmark for miles. We drop down from the wonderful viewpoint to the valley where the meandering infant river Alne flows between lush meadows, and on the way pass close to the splendid Umberslade Children's Farm. Beyond Danzey Green we can see the extensive Mockley Woods which have a colourful floor of bluebells in springtime. The return to Tanworth takes us near Forde Hall and over farmland, a final climb extending the beautiful views with every step.

PLACES of INTEREST

A mile from Tanworth-in-Arden along the drive to Umberslade is the **Umberslade Children's Farm**. Here youngsters can meet a great assortment of animals and birds. There are demonstrations of country crafts and fun rides over the countryside on a tractor-drawn cart. The farm is open daily. **Earlswood Lakes** are 3 miles to the north of Tanworth along country lanes. These were constructed to 'top-up' the nearby Stratford-upon-Avon Canal. Sailors and anglers find good sport here and it is pleasant to stroll through the woods which border the banks. There is also a farm selling delicious ice cream!

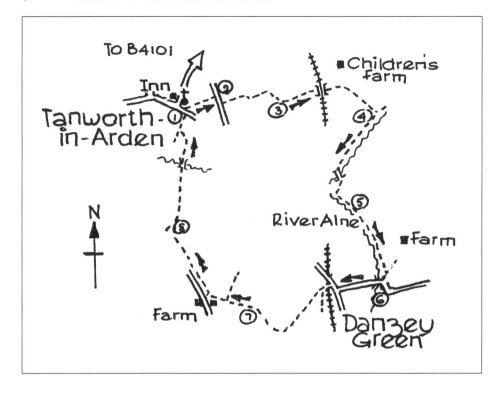

❹ At the far hedge is a waymark post. Turn right to follow near a left-hand stream to a footbridge. Go over the water. Two paths are now indicated. Take the left-hand path to a step stile. Follow the little right-hand river.

❺ Go around a corner to a gate and double stile. Here two paths are arrowed. Take the right-hand way. A series of stiles (some waymarked) and gates now shows the way (never far from the right-hand little river) to a stile onto a farm drive. Turn right to a lane. Turn right.

❻ Follow the lane to a T-junction. At once turn right then immediately left. The farm 'road' goes over a railway. After 400 yards the way divides into three. Keep ahead through a metal gate alongside a right-hand hedge. Away to the left are Mockley Woods. Pass through a metal corner gate and follow the track around the edge of the field to another gate.

❼ The wide track now hugs the borders of arable lands to a farm and lane. The manor house here was granted to Roger de la Forde by John de Somery of Aspley. Do not enter the lane but turn right over a stile. Climb the hill alongside the left-hand hedge and lane. Near the summit bear right to a stile to the right of a wood. Keep ahead by the wood (now on the left) to another path. Turn right.

❽ Drop down at the borders of two fields. In a corner go a yard or two right and cross a rather hidden bridge. In a field walk by a left-hand border to a corner stile. Over this turn left. The path leads to a lane and Tanworth is just to the left.

The village green with its spreading chestnut tree.

ULLENHALL

Length: 3½ miles

Getting there: Turn off the A4189 between Redditch and Henley-in-Arden, signed 'Ullenhall'.	**Parking:** There is a layby on the lane opposite the church.	**Maps:** OS Landranger – Worcester (150) and Stratford-upon-Avon (151). (GR 121672).

Like so many villages in recent years Ullenhall has lost many of its traditional ingredients. Walk along the main street and you will see houses that were once shops, and the post office, school and vicarage are no more. But there is still a village pub and a fine village hall. The old blacksmith's forge is a private house these days but note the fine weathervane depicting the old craft. There are many pleasant modern houses mixed with the old timber-framed dwellings and red-brick cottages from earlier centuries. At the Domesday survey Ullenhall was spelt Ulenhala – Ula's halh or the Saxon Ula's valley – and around the village there is much evidence of the medieval ridge and furrow farming.

It remains a quiet village today with an air of 'away from it all'. This must have appealed to William Booth (a noted hanged (at the third attempt by the hangman) for the then capital offence of forgery.

Another of Ullenhall's infamous residents in the past was Lady Luxborough. She was spirited away to the seclusion of the countryside from London by her husband, Robert Knight, in 1736. She herself stated that her conduct with an admirer poet was 'more than prudence or decency allows' but the banishment from the bright lights did not dim her zest for living. At her home called Barrells (which lies in ruins after a fire in 1933) Lady Luxborough gathered around her many literary figures – and her ghost still enjoys the old house in the wood.

forger) in the early 19th century. Although he was acquitted of his brother's murder at the isolated Hall End Farm (which we pass on the walk) he was duly

Inquisitive horses guarding the stile in Ullenhall.

The walk starts from St Mary's church. This is the new St Mary's and was built in 1875, replacing the building some ½ mile away which was the centre of the village until the plague. We then continue along the main street, once so bustling with many shops and even a café. Over the fields the hamlet of Blunt's Green is reached, south of which we pass the notorious Hall End Farm before climbing the ridge to what remains of Ullenhall's former church. There are some pleasant field paths back to the village which, remember, still has its welcoming pub.

THE WALK

❶ From the layby opposite the church go through the metal kissing-gate. There is a clear, well-walked track over the sheep pasture to the road. Turn right to pass the old forge building. Bear left at the war memorial to another junction.

❷ Turn left along Watery Lane – appropriately named as usually water tumbles alongside. At a road junction go left then immediately right through a kissing-gate. In the pasture walk alongside the right-hand border. Through a corner gate keep ahead (left-hand hedge) to a stile (nibbled by horses) onto a lane.

❸ Cross to the opposite stile and follow the arrowed direction to a stile just to the right of a metal gate. Bear right and, aiming just to the right of a cottage, make for a stile onto a lane. Turn right a step or two then take a signed path over a stile, left.

❹ Within a couple of yards there is another stile with two paths arrowed. Take

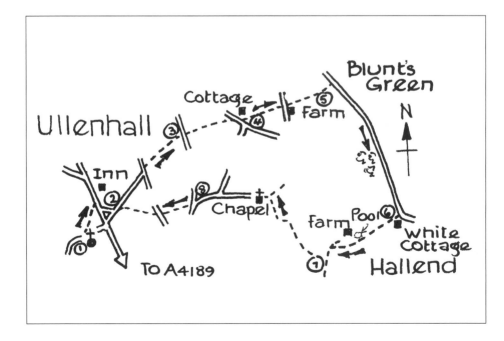

the direction of the right-hand one to a far metal gate onto a lane. Cross to the opposite stile and path and take the direction indicated to climb another stile. Bear slightly right to climb the ridge to a stile (the right-hand one of two) which is tucked in a corner.

❺ In the next field walk by a pond to a stile by a white cottage. Follow the fenced path to a lane at Blunt's Green. Turn right. You may hear trains here as the North Warwickshire line runs on an embankment to the left. Built in 1912, the branch line to Stratford managed to escape the Beeching cuts and many subsequent threats to axe it. Keep on the lane for about ⅔ mile. As the lane turns sharp left turn right by a white cottage. The bridleway is signed through a gate.

❻ Follow the bridleway through further field gates and through a hunting gate. Keep ahead to pass a pool. Keep the farmstead of Hall End Farm and barns on your right and continue to a gate in the far right-hand corner of the meadow. On the farm drive keep ahead. Climb to a step stile on the right to an often arable field.

❼ Follow the arrowed direction to a stile (difficult for dogs!) in a corner. In a pasture climb the rise to a stile into a churchyard, left. Go past the chapel that was once the old village church to a gate onto a lane. Follow the lane to a junction. Keep ahead to the next junction (Moat Farm Lane).

❽ Cross to the path through the opposite gate. Follow the path through the length of the pasture to a lane. Cross to the opposite path through a gate. A clear path leads to Watery Lane. Turn left. Keep ahead at a junction to a T-junction. Go left, then right. Church Hill leads back to Ullenhall church.

LONG ITCHINGTON

Length: 3 miles

| Getting there: The village is on the A423 (Coventry to Banbury road) 10 miles from Coventry. | Parking: Roadside in the Square near the church. | Map: OS Landranger – Stratford-upon-Avon (151). (GR 413652). |

The place has nothing to do with an itch but takes its name from being on the tiny river Itchen, a tributary of the Avon. Long Itchington has a place in the history books for it is the birthplace of St Wufstan who was one of Britain's first statesman. (Others would say he demonstrated the virtues of appeasement as he was the only bishop to collaborate with the Norman invaders and was rewarded by becoming Bishop of Worcester!)

Near the village pond where swans take up residence is the magnificent timber-framed Tudor House. Queen Elizabeth I would have seen this mansion when (invited by the grand-daughter of Dudley, Earl of Leicester) she came to feast in a great tent 'which for number and shift of large and goodely rooms might be comparable with a beautiful pallais'.

FOOD and DRINK

On this walk there is a veritable feast of pubs, all very welcoming and all with a wonderful choice of meals. The Harvester in Long Itchington's central Square is especially proud of its beers – the guest ale on my visit was the intriguing Judge's Solicitor's Ruin! Also in the village are the Green Man and the Jolly Fisherman, opposite the village pond, which was offering 'free food for kids' when I was there. On joining the towing path of the canal there are inns on each bank. Both are bedecked with flowers in summer and have well-maintained gardens where one could pass the time by idly watching the boats go by. At each of the next two road bridges there are pretty pubs. The first is the Blue Lias Inn – the name comes from the type of stone which is the raw material for the local cement works. The route then leaves the waterway by the Boat Inn. You are not advised to visit all the hostelries in one go – unless someone else is driving you home!

The church (Holy Trinity) has an unusual tower as it carries the stump of a spire; the pinnacle tumbled during a service in 1762 when it was struck by lightning. Inside the church is an oak screen which was set in place over 600 years ago.

The village has pleasant, tree-fringed greens and a nice mix of old timbered and thatched cottages and modern houses. There is a cluster of shops and inns (see left).

From the Square the walk crosses a contributory brook to the river Itchen then, beyond a meadow where there are the ridges and furrows of medieval strip farming, joins the towing path of the Grand Union Canal and climbs the Stock-

Narrow boats on the canal.

ton Flight. We return to the village along narrow lanes where there are only a couple of farmsteads and along which few cars venture. There are views over a gentle countryside of low, wooded hills and mixed farmlands.

THE WALK

❶ From the Square walk along the nearby Thorn Way which is signed as a 'no through road'. Just after the lane twists sharply left (and opposite a garden pump) a path is signed over a stile on the right. There is rather a profusion of arrows but take a direction in the pasture to the left of a distant chimney.

❷ Climb a stile and go over a brick footbridge. In a pasture walk to the far left corner. Climb the stile and proceed to the canal towing path. The waterway got its

name in 1929 when many old canal navigations were amalgamated. A great amount of money was spent during the 1930s when it was widened along its 140 miles to accommodate larger commercial craft. There are still boats carrying coal but the Grand Union Canal is now a popular holiday waterway. Turn left to go under the road.

❸ Walk alongside the canal and beside the locks of the Stockton Flight. Not far away are great cement factories and we pass crumbling chimneys of old industrial works. Go under a lane. At the next bridge (A426) leave the waterway. Turn left along the lane.

❹ After ¾ mile there is a crossroads. Turn left along the lane signed to Long Itchington. Within a mile and by right-hand allotments the lane bends sharp left (a

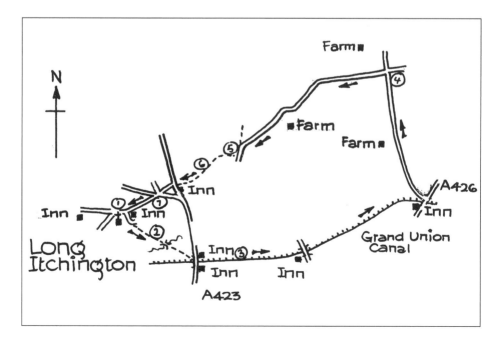

footpath is signed here which you ignore). About 50 yards further take another signed path over a stile, right.

❺ In a sometimes sown field walk by the right-hand border. Go a few yards around the far corner to a rather hidden bridge and stile. At once climb another stile to a large pasture.

❻ Follow the right-hand boundary. Towards the far corner go through a hedge gap. Regain the old direction (with the hedge now on the left side). Go over a stile and adjoining a gate to a vehicle way to a road. Cross and turn left. Within a step or two turn right so the village pond is on your right.

❼ After 100 yards turn left. Church Road leads to the Square at Long Itchington.

A canalside pub.

NAPTON-ON-THE-HILL

Length: 4½ miles

Getting there: Napton-on-the-Hill is just off the A425 about midway between Leamington Spa and Daventry.	Parking: Quiet roadsides in the village centre.	Map: OS Landranger – Stratford-upon-Avon (151). (GR 465611).

The addition 'on-the-Hill' is actually superfluous as the name is from the Anglo-Saxon 'hnaepp' or 'village on the hilltop'. It is high above the plain through which the sinuous Oxford Canal was constructed over 200 years ago. It is said seven counties can be seen from the breezy 500 ft height.

The founders of our ancient churches loved to build on lofty places to be as near as possible to heaven. Napton was no exception and this was a large community in medieval times – in fact the third largest town in Warwickshire. It was a great agricultural region and it had those marks of respectability and size granted by Royal Charter – a weekly market and annual fair. Although these have long

FOOD and DRINK

The inn on the green is a typical village pub, offering good, traditional fare, including an excellent ploughman's platter. To sit outside and watch the rural scene unfolding is a simple delight. The Folly, on the route, is near the waterway and is popular with holidaymakers. It has built up a reputation for its pies. Napton has a well-stocked village shop which will sell those essential provisions for a picnic on the walk. The waterside shop, passed later, supplies customers who travel along the canal – and will also satisfy thirsty and hungry walkers!

since been abandoned the population has remained remarkably constant at around 1,000 inhabitants.

A feature of Napton is the finely restored windmill which crowns the hill. There has been a mill on the site for many centuries – the present one is recorded as far back as 1543.

The walk starts at the green with its traditional spreading chestnut tree where cottages with dipping thatch and the inn once witnessed the bustle of markets and fairs. The route drops down to the pastures below the village and then visits the hamlet of Chapel Green, whose 14th-century chapel is no more. The return is along the towing path of the Oxford Canal. There is a beautifully sited canalside pub and a nearby shop for delicious ices. We climb a final steep ascent to the 'on-the-hill' village, passing the windmill and then the church with its traditional avenue of lime trees up to the Norman doorway.

THE WALK

❶   From the village green climb the gentle rise of High Street which becomes Hackwell Street. At the junction with School Hill there is a path signed by a barn on the right. Go down steps and climb a stile to a meadow.

❷   Follow the signed direction to go over a corner stile. Keep downhill to a rather hidden stile to a vehicle track. Turn right. At a road keep the direction to pass a sign, 'Dog Lane'. A step or two further on take a signed bridleway down a vehicle track left.

❸   After ⅓ mile the vehicle track veers left. Maintain the old heading to pass through a metal gate to a pasture. Walk alongside a right-hand hedge.

❹   Go through a corner gate and continue by right-hand hedges and fences. As the field boundary bears left go through a metal gate. (You may find the arrow a little confusing!) Continue by the old hedge which is now on your left side.

PLACES of INTEREST

Near the church is the fascinating **Church Leyes Farm**. It is advertised as being 'In harmony with Nature' and this is just what it is, a simple, basic farm which loves to share its joys with visitors. There are no unusual animals but just sheep, cattle, free-range hens, geese and of course Bert the Turkey, and footpaths along which to wander and observe the wildlife. The farm is open every day except Saturdays. **Draycote Water Country Park**, 6 miles to the north, is based on a 240 hectare reservoir which since its construction has attracted a wide variety of wildfowl. It also attracts trout fishermen and yachtsmen but this is essentially a wonderful, peaceful spot and ideal for a picnic with benches and tables provided. Nearby are the Draycote Meadows which support many ancient grasses and wildflowers.

The windmill at Napton-on-the-Hill.

Within 100 yards go through an old corner gateway (the gate may be missing). At once turn right to a bridle gate now seen.

❺ Maintain the direction in the next pasture to go through a corner metal gate. Immediately turn right to walk past a pool. Continue to a lane. Turn right and pass a junction. Within ¼ mile turn left at the private drive of a house called Eureka which is also a public right of way.

❻ Through the gate, follow the drive for a few steps. The path is then well way-marked to pass behind garages and over a stile. Turn left and walk down the centre of a large pasture. Over a bridge bear left

to a gate in the far left corner to a lane. Turn right. Cross the canal and at once go left to the towing path. Turn left to pass under the lane.

❼ Follow the canal, passing locks, shop and inn. This is a popular waterway for holiday sailors although during some dry summers there is a shortage of water. It is a contour canal where the engineers followed a level course where possible but this resulted in a twisting route to skirt around uplands. So we find a way slow and tortuous for the old commercial traffic but so relaxing and unhurried in today's world. At bridge 112 leave the canal. Go over the bridge. Within 100 yards take a signed

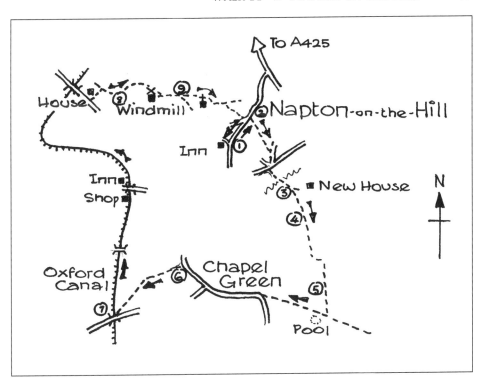

path, left. Walk alongside a garden to a vehicle way. Turn right for 20 yards then follow the way left (arrow on post) alongside a wire fence.

❽ The path goes along the ridge left which is above a grassed-over clay quarry. The quarries here for many years provided work for the locals (and clay for the nearby brickworks). We are now making for a point to the left of houses and the windmill. Climb a stile tucked into a corner and walk along a fenced way to a house drive. Turn left. When the vehicle way divides take the left-hand way.

❾ Pass Church Leyes Farm and the church of St Lawrence, which has many stones laid in the 12th century. The prominent tower was an 18th-century addition. Some 150 yards further turn right along an unsigned tarmac path to Hackwell Street. Turn right to retrace your steps to the village green.

ASTON CANTLOW

Length: 4 miles

Getting there: From the A3400 at Wootton Wawen take the B4089 south-west. Within 2 miles take signed lanes to Aston Cantlow.	Parking: There is a quiet road in front of the pub.	Map: OS Landranger – Stratford-upon-Avon (151). (GR 139599).

This is a small village of only a few hundred people but it might have been so very different. The Norman lord William de Cantilupe (from Canteloup in Normandy) built a grand castle using the waters of the little river Alne for his moat. From 1227 he possessed that most valued of favours from the monarch – the right to hold a weekly market and annual fair. William was ambitious but unfortunately the competition from the equally ambitious de Montforts down the highway at Henley was too great. Henley prospered and Aston Cantlow remained a sleepy little village.

The peace also might have been disturbed by modern-day tourists on the

---

FOOD and DRINK

The 16th-century inn, the King's Head, is so picturesque with wisteria appearing to tumble down from the eaves. I can vouch that the meals are really home-made as I chatted with the landlord's wife in the kitchen whilst she cooked the day's 'specials' – I like to think of myself as something of a curry connoisseur and the Singapore Recipe Curry was truly delicious. Also on the stove was the Bobotie, a popular spicy meat loaf from South Africa.

Shakespeare trail. It is said that John Shakespeare took Mary Arden from Wilmcote in 1557 to be married at the church of St John the Baptist (built of blue-lias limestone hewn from the local Rough Hills). Their son William was born in 1564. Unfortunately there are no records from those far off days to verify the facts and no registers for potential tourists to examine.

Opposite the pub is the timber-framed Guild House which dates from the 16th century. A religious order – the Guild of St Mary – was based here. Many of the ancient buildings, like the mill which made paper and needles and the chapel in Chapel Lane, have long gone but there are still plenty of lovely old cottages and houses.

The route soon crosses the disused GWR railway. Built in 1876 it was affectionately known as the coffee-pot line because of the distinctive funnels of the engines. We then follow the bank of the river Alne, where the willows dip low over the water and can hide the elusive and beautiful kingfisher. Through the hamlet of Little Alne craft workshops are passed then there is a gentle climb up the aptly

named Round Hill, rewarded by a splendid view. Down the other side we go over a pasture with the ridges and furrows of medieval strip farming. Here we are on the route of the Monarch's Way – a long distance path which traces the circuitous journeys of Charles I. The return leg of our walk follows the valley of the river through lush water meadows and rich arable lands.

THE WALK

❶ The route starts from the pub near the church. Walk along the main street and turn left down Chapel Lane. At the end keep ahead along a stony vehicle way. Climb a stile and walk alongside a left-hand fence. There is a corner stile to cross the old rail route then go over another stile to a meadow.

PLACES of INTEREST

The Stratford-upon-Avon Canal crosses the lane 2 miles to the east of Aston Cantlow. The interesting thing is that it does this over a spectacular, high aqueduct. There are 13 brick piers which have carried the metal canal troughs since 1813. At **Wilmcote**, 2 miles south-east of the village, is the house which was the home of William Shakespeare's mother, Mary Arden. The old farmhouse contains many fascinating rural and agricultural bygones and is open daily. **Ragley Hall** is 5 miles to the south-west. This 17th-century mansion is the family seat of the Marquis of Hertford and has an elegant Ionic portico by James Watt. The gardens were designed by 'Capability' Brown in the middle of the 18th century (they now include an exciting adventure playground). Of especial interest in the house is the modern mural which features present-day members of the family. The house, the park with its nature walk and the gardens are open daily except during the winter months.

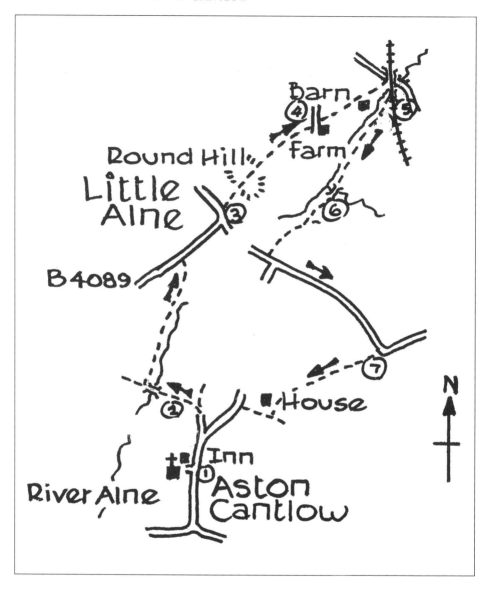

❷ Two paths are signed. Take the left-hand path to walk directly over the field to a railed footbridge across the river. Turn right and walk alongside the river. Not only may you be lucky enough to spot a kingfisher but the yellow 'cup-and-saucer'

water lily also likes this habitat. The path goes around a large field to a stile to the B4089. Turn right through Little Alne.

❸ There is a road junction and the B4089 twists sharp left. At once go over a

The spectacular canal aqueduct dating from 1813.

stile, right. Follow the left-hand border to a corner stile. Maintain the direction up Round Hill to a ridge-top stile. Drop down the slope (ridges and furrows can be seen in the meadows and you are now on the waymarked Monarch's Way) making for a point just to the left of a red-brick farm complex. Climb a fence stile to a lane.

❹ Turn left then at once right over a stile to a pasture. Pass just to the left of a brick barn and keep ahead to a far corner stile to a lane. Turn right. Pass under a railway and over the river. Immediately turn right to again pass under the railway then climb a stile to a pasture. This is a railway that still operates. The North Warwickshire line, built in 1908, has been under constant threat since the Beeching era but is still a wonderful escape route into the countryside.

❺ Follow the arrowed way to pass through an obsolete gateway. At once turn left. Walk the length of the pasture, gradually nearing the right-hand river. Follow the river, going along a path through trees. Emerging in a pasture, keep ahead to the far stile now seen. Go over a railed footbridge across a brook.

❻ Walk straight down a rough pasture to a gate and fence stile to a tractor way. Turn left to join a bolder track (once the way to a railway goods yard). Turn right to a lane. Turn left to pass a junction. Within ½ mile the road bends sharp left. Go right through a metal gate (the footpath sign is hidden).

❼   Walk alongside a right-hand hedge. Go through a corner gap and continue alongside a hedge. Just past a house go through another gap. Take care – the plank bridge over a ditch may be overgrown. On a farm drive turn right to a lane. Turn left to Aston Cantlow.

SNITTERFIELD

Length: 4½ miles

Getting there: Turn off the A439, northwards, 1½ miles from Stratford-upon-Avon. The village can also be reached from the A46, following the Snitterfield signs.	Parking: On quiet roadsides near the crossroads by the village pubs.	Map: OS Landranger – Stratford-upon-Avon (151). (GR 213599).

Snitterfield is a pretty village – it is close to Stratford but is virtually ignored by visitors on the 'tourist trail'. But how different things might have been. . . In the churchyard lie Richard Shakespeare and his wife in unknown graves. Richard's son John was ambitious and in 1551 went on to make his fortune in the town. He married Mary Arden and a son William was born. The rest as they say is history. There were few records of property in those far off days, but a lady in a cottage near the church is adamant that the Tudor building in her garden was the old farmhouse of the Shake-

FOOD and DRINK

There are two good pubs in Snitterfield; they are close together and a pleasant contrast. The Fox-hunter is a freehouse and is covered in beautiful hanging baskets in summertime. There are plenty of benches and tables at the front where you can watch the world pass by. The other is the Snitterfield Arms, which has a pleasant garden. An excellent Sunday roast is on offer in both establishments. Snitterfield's village store has re-opened after a period of closure. Here you can buy provisions for a picnic meal on the route – or chocolates (say) as a reward at the end of the walk!

The unusual name is from the Anglo-Saxon 'the place of the snipe'. The bird has long since gone but the lowlands which it loved remain. They are now drained by the little Sherbourne Brook that flows into the Avon and pleasant footpaths cross them.

The church is from the 13th and 14th centuries and is noted for its stained-glass windows, especially one depicting four Saxon bishops and saints. There are also monuments to the Philips family who were members of Parliament and great benefactors and up to the First World War owned much of Snitterfield.

The walk passes old timber-framed cottages to a path over fields showing the ridges and furrows of the ancient strip speares. If it could be proved then the peace of Snitterfield would be severely tested by the tourists. But the village still sleeps. . .

A welcome seat.

farming. The way then hugs the placid Sherbourne Brook and little lanes lead to the busy route into Stratford but we soon leave the hubbub behind over arable fields. The return gives a splendid view across the valley to where an obelisk is prominent. This is on a hill near the Philips' home (now the Welcombe Hotel) and is in memory of Mark who was 'a good wise and brave man, a friend of liberty in evil days'. As we enter Snitterfield again we go near the possible Shakespeare home and the church.

THE WALK
❶ From the crossroads by the inns follow the road by the Foxhunter. Within 400 yards the road (Wolverton Road) swings

sharp left. Keep ahead along a lane signed as a 'no through road' to pass cottages.

❷ The lane becomes a footpath. Pass through a kissing-gate and maintain the direction through meadows (some ridged and furrowed) to a farm 'road'. Turn right then at once left. The path goes alongside the hidden Sherbourne Brook to emerge on a lane near a waterworks. Turn left.

❸ Within 300 yards turn right through a metal kissing-gate. Immediately turn left. We again follow the edge of the brook (now on the right side). At a railed bridge cross the water. At once turn left to regain the old direction (but now with the brook on the left).

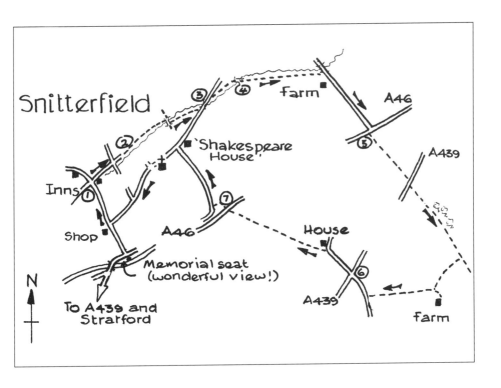

PLACES of INTEREST

Charlecote Park is 4 miles along lanes south-west of Snitterfield. This grand house and park were given to the National Trust by Sir Montgomerie Fairfax-Lucy in 1945 – the property had been in the Lucy family since the 12th century. Legend has it that the young Will Shakespeare was caught poaching deer there. The gardens were improved by 'Capability' Brown in the 1760s and deer still roam in the lovely park. Charlecote is open from May to the end of September (with limited opening in April and October). **Hatton Craft Centre** is 5 miles north of the village. Many country crafts are demonstrated and goods are for sale. There are animals to see and a fascinating nature trail. Refreshments are available.

❹ Go over a waymarked stile and follow the arrowed way. Keep ahead at a marked post (still by the brook). Pass through a kissing-gate and follow the path to a lane. Turn right to the A46. Turn right a step or two then cross the busy road to pass through a metal gate.

❺ The bridleway follows a tractor way to the A439. Cross to the signed way opposite. In an arable field walk by a left-hand hedge. At a corner turn right to walk alongside the left-hand hedge to a farm drive. Turn right to a lane – fine view now across the valley. Turn right to the main road.

❻ Cross to the opposite lane. Follow the lane for ⅓ mile. As the lane bends right take a signed path left. The path is near the right-hand garden. Continue to an often large arable field. Take arrowed heading over the open field to the A46.

❼ Cross to the signed cycle way opposite. This leads to a lane. Turn right. At a T-junction turn left. (The 'Shakespeare house' is just to the right.) The road goes past the church. Keep ahead at junctions to a T-junction. A memorial seat with a wonderful view is a little way to the left and is well worth the short detour. Turn right to return to the crossroads and pubs.

HARBURY

Length: 6 miles

Getting there: 4 miles south-east of Leamington Spa on the A425 take the B4452 to Harbury.	Parking: Quiet roadsides.	Map: OS Landranger – Stratford-upon-Avon (151). (GR 373600).

There is much history in Harbury. Fossils of dinosaurs were found in quarries here and now reside in the Natural History Museum at South Kensington; the Iron Age is represented by traces of a fort; and the Romans took their great highway of the Fosse Way near the village.

Overlooking Harbury is the tower of a tall windmill, now sadly minus its sails which struck and killed the miller. His ghost, of course, has often been seen. Further along the High Street is the Norman church of All Saints – its tower feels its 13th-century age and its lean is now solidly buttressed.

The ancient manor was once owned by the Wagstaffe family and there are many reminders of that era. The Wagstaffe School near the church (now a house) took its first scholars in 1611 and there are

Wagstaffe memorials in the church. Earlier the Knights Templars owned the lands and are remembered in the names of Temple House and Temple End.

The network of narrow streets in the village contain many little cottages of cream-hued lias stone. They often have steep roofs, indicating that they were once thatched.

After leaving the village centre we go along Temple End then over lush pastures. The walk goes near the site of a great house, the former seat of the Peyto family, who are remembered in the splendour of Chesterton church. Their tombs are wonderful examples of the art of alabaster carving. Near the Fosse Way the route is alongside the 8-acre site of a Roman posting station. The area is grassed and is said to be unexcavated and still retaining its secrets. We return to Harbury after visiting the beautifully restored Peyto windmill on a gentle hilltop.

THE WALK
❶ From the High Street walk away from the church and along Mill Street with the tower of the ancient windmill behind cottages on the right. Turn left down Farm Street. At a T-junction (inn nearby) turn right.

❷ At the end of houses on the left (Temple End) climb a stile to a pasture. Walk by a fence and climb a corner stile. Maintain the heading in an arable field by a left-hand border. Keep a constant heading with a series of stiles to show the way through meadows to a lane.

❸ Turn right then at once left. The bridleway is shown over a bridge and through a hunting gate. The right of way now cuts over open fields, aiming for a point to the right of a distant brick wall and cottage. (The fields are arable and if the going is difficult keep to the border.) To the right of the brick wall pass through a metal gate.

❹ At once turn left to pass through a bridle gate to a pasture. Two ways are arrowed. Take the direction of the footpath (yellow arrow). The brick wall, left, indicates the site of the Peyto mansion,

The windmill tower at Harbury.

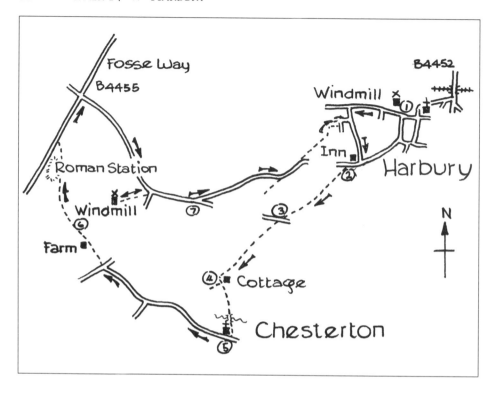

demolished in 1802 when misfortune struck the family. The path goes diagonally over the field to cross a brook. Continue to follow the waymarked route through the churchyard of Chesterton church to a lane. In the churchyard is a fine brick gateway; designed by Inigo Jones it once was the way to the great house. Now it leads nowhere.

❺ Turn right. Follow the lane through Chesterton and keep ahead past a junction to a T-junction. Cross to the signed bridle-way through a metal gate. Follow the farm drive and keep to the right of the farmstead and barns. Beyond, stay on a bold tractor way with a hedge on the left side.

❻ Pass through a far corner metal gate.

The tractor way goes right, then left with the unploughed area to the left marking the Roman posting station. On the busy Fosse Way turn right to a crossroads. Turn right. At a junction take the path to the Peyto windmill. This treasure was built in 1632 and is also the work of Inigo Jones. Return to the main road and continue along it to the right, bearing left at a junction.

❼ About ½ mile further the road twists sharp left then right. Here take a signed path over a stile, left. Take the arrowed direction to climb to a stile. Follow the fenced path around gardens (beware of stinging nettles in summer). At an estate road turn left then go right at a T-junction. This leads to Binswood Road and Harbury village centre.

PRIORS MARSTON

Length: 3 miles

Getting there: 10 miles south-east of Leamington Spa along the A425 take a gated lane, south, to Priors Marston.	Parking: There is a quiet road-side near the green and war memorial.	Map: OS Landranger – Stratford-upon-Avon (151). (GR 489573).

This walk from Priors Marston is to the Warwickshire borderlands – and in fact trespasses into Northamptonshire on the route. These are limestone uplands and in days long past the rusty-hued stone supplied the handy building material for the village, which was declared a conservation area in 1972 because of its magnificent buildings. Many date from the 17th cen-

tury and were houses on the estate of the Earls Spencer. The Earl is still Lord of the Manor.

The gem in the crown is the lovely church of St Leonard, approached along pathways of blue bricks (which were once made in the local brickworks). There are ancient traditional yews nudging the church, the oldest part of which is from the 13th century.

There is no sign of the residence of the priors who gave the village the first part of its name. They came from the Benedictine Priory of Coventry but they were dispersed after the Dissolution in 1539. There is still Priory Farm where one of the fields (now called Bury Yard) was once a monks' graveyard.

The trim village green is the starting point for the walk; here there is a stout plinth which is the war memorial. The 'Welsh Road' passes this spot – it was the route along which the drovers took their cattle on the way from the Welsh borders to the markets of London.

Early on the walk we go up the wooded ridge which overlooks the village. Then there are pleasant bridleways through mixed farmlands and a crossing (without formalities!) over the border. The return leg starts by hugging the edge of a golf course. The views overlooking the artificial lakes in the valley are truly magnificent –

almost convincing a rambler to become a golfer! The final paths are across the fields of Priory Farm where the farmer takes great care to ensure that the rights of way are kept clear and a pleasure to walk.

THE WALK

❶ From the village green and the war memorial walk along the nearby Hellidon Road. At the junction by the Falcon Inn turn along the lane, left, then pass the Holly Bush Inn. At a junction keep ahead to follow a paved path into the church-yard. There are some fine stained glass windows to be seen and plenty of evidence of the church's Norman builders.

❷ Keep the church on your left side and continue to a gate out of the churchyard. Maintain the heading past a thatched cottage to a lane. Turn right. Within 150

The 13th-century church at Priors Marston.

yards the lane twists left. Climb a stile on the right. Follow the shaded pathway to a stile to a rough pasture.

❸ Turn left and walk uphill. Keep ahead over a stile and up steps to reach a far corner stile onto a lane. Cross to the signed bridleway opposite. Go past an old farmstead then walk along a sunken tractor way. Maintain the direction to pass through gateways and gates.

❹ The arrowed way goes just to the right of a farm to join the farm drive. Within a few yards the drive goes sharp right. Keep the old direction through a metal gate and alongside a left-hand hedge. Pass through

further gates to reach a lane. Turn left.

❺ Within 300 yards and just before the entrance to Hellidon Lakes Club take a signed bridleway through a gate, left. Walk beside the left-hand border of a golf course fairway and by the hedge.

❻ Maintain the heading by the golf course for about ½ mile. Pass out of the course through a metal gate to arable lands and along a tractor way by the left-hand hedge which soon bears right. Look out for the place where the tractor way and the bridleway veer left away from the border of the field to pass through rough scrubland.

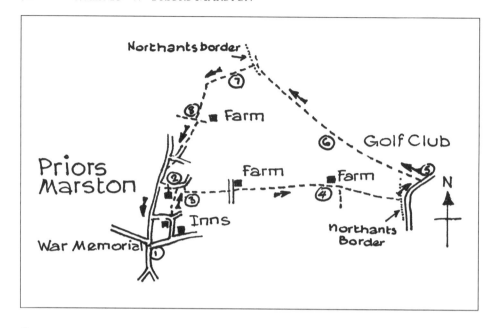

❼ Go through a gap to another field. Turn left to walk alongside a left-hand hedge. The hedge and the bridleway bear right to a hedge gap and a signpost. Turn left along a signed path over an open field. Go through a gap to the next field. Keep ahead. Half-way across the field turn 90 degrees left and aim for a point 30 yards to the right of a barn.

❽ Continue to a stile to the farm drive. Turn left towards the house, Priory Farm. Within a step or two turn right through a metal gate. Take the arrowed direction over the open field to pass through a metal gate to a cul-de-sac lane. Walk to a junction. Cross to the opposite path and continue to a road. The village green is to the left.

BIDFORD-ON-AVON

Length: 4½ miles

Getting there: Bidford is halfway between Stratford-upon-Avon and Evesham on the B439.	Parking: There is a car park by the river Avon off the B4085.	Map: OS Landranger – Worcester (150). (GR 099519).

My dictionary is not very definite about a village – it is 'larger than a hamlet and smaller than a town'. Bidford is of some size – around 2,000 inhabitants – but I still consider that it qualifies for this book as a 'large village'.

Shakespeare knew the place as a favourite drinking haunt and in some doggerel on Warwickshire villages it was called 'Drunken Bidford' – his Falcon Inn still stands but is no longer a pub. The Romans too came here as they took their Ryknild Street across the river by means of a ford at Bidford (Byda's Ford in Saxon times). There is a pub called the Anglo-Saxon and I remember that when a car park was constructed not so long ago an Anglo-Saxon burial ground was found.

village for 700 years although it is generally accepted that the interior of the building has been somewhat tarnished by over-zealous Victorian restorers.

Further downstream are the eight arches of the stone bridge over the Avon. This dates from the 15th century and was partially destroyed during the Civil War. It finds difficulty coping with today's impatient traffic.

Increased traffic also passes under the bridge since the river navigation was reopened following extensive work a few years ago. The colourful holiday craft and the swans gliding between the reeds are seen by many visitors as the meadows at Bidford are a favourite venue for folk from

The tower of the parish church (dedicated to St Laurence) has overlooked the

The Falcon, (once a pub) was a favourite with Shakespeare.

the towns. Here you can relax after the walk and watch cricket or football games.

There is a nice path over the fields at the start of the walk to the hamlet at Barton. Here we find cottages capped by thatch and an inn which tumbles with pretty flowers in summertime. The route continues over clear paths across mainly arable farmland. Past a wood where game birds scatter as we approach we reach the multi-gabled Bickmarsh Hall. The hamlet has a scattering of houses in market garden land – look out for plums growing virtually wild beside the lane during the summer months! We return to Bidford on the Avon Valley Footpath from Marlcliff, where there is a lovely garden open to the public.

THE WALK

❶ From the car park by the bridge cross the B4085 to a step stile onto rough pastureland. The clear path goes diagonally over the field to a distant stile. Maintain the heading over a sometimes

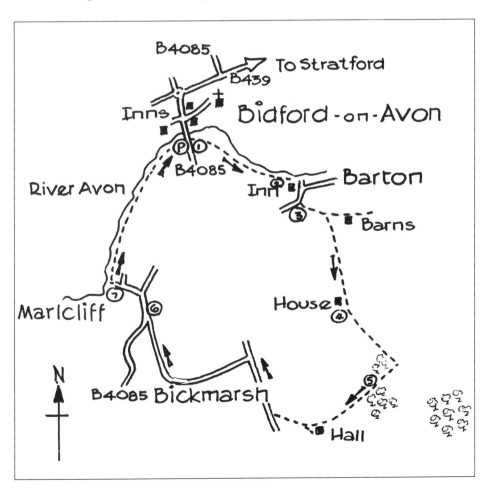

arable field to a stile on a flood-prevention bank. The path is along the bank to a river weir.

❷ The clear track swings right to a stile onto a lane at Barton. Follow this for a step or two to a junction. Keep ahead along the road for a few yards.

❸ As the road twists right keep ahead along a stony farm road. Within 300 yards there is a junction of farm roads. Take the 'road' right – signed 'Private Road' but it is a right of way footpath. Go past a house along a tractor way which picks up a right-hand hedge.

❹ The tractor way becomes a footpath (still with a right-hand hedge) then the path is alongside a line of newly planted sapling trees to a clump of trees. Turn right – the path is arrowed on a tree and points over the open field to the corner of a wood.

❺ Keep the wood on your left to join the drive of the farm of Bickmarsh Hall to a road. Turn right for about 400 yards. Turn left down Sixteen Acres Lane at Bickmarsh. Follow the lane to a junction with the B4085 at Marlcliff.

PLACES of INTEREST

Near the route of the walk at **Bickmarsh** is a gliding club. It is fascinating to watch these huge, silent 'birds' soaring into the sky. There are trial flights available if you want to be part of the action. To the south and west of Bidford is the **Vale of Evesham**. This area is the market garden of the Midlands and during all seasons of the year there are many roadside stalls selling fruit and vegetables. It is especially lovely at late springtime when 'blossom routes' are signposted through the lanes.

---

❻ Keep ahead along the B4085 for a few steps. As the main road twists sharp right keep ahead along the lane (The Bank), signed as a 'no through road'. When the lane divides take the left-hand stony way past a garden open to the public.

❼ Just before a fishermen's car park turn right to climb a stile to a pasture. We now walk along the path beside the river – Marlcliff is at the end of a pleasant 9-mile riverside walk (the Avon Valley Footpath) from Stratford. This returns us to the riverside meadows and car park.

RADWAY

Length: 3½ miles

Getting there: 7 miles north-west of Banbury along the A422 turn northwards along a lane signed to Radway.

Parking: There are quiet road-sides in the centre of the village.

Map: OS Landranger – Stratford-upon-Avon (151). (GR 369481).

Radway is a village of brown Horton stone cottages; there is no shop or inn but it is a place of great importance in the history of our land.

It was on Sunday, 23rd October 1642 that the troops of the king rode by on their way to the first battle of the Civil War. The site of the indecisive conflict in which many thousands were slain is actu-ally a mile north-west of Radway (unfortunately it cannot be visited these days).

The church we see today was rebuilt in a new position in 1866. Opposite is another historic building – Radway Grange – which has trees planted by the famous 18th-century parliamentarian Lord Chatham. The house was owned by the Gothic Revival architect Sanderson

FOOD and DRINK

The Rose and Crown in Ratley was a real rustic hostelry until 20 years ago – I can remember when all the beer was served from jugs through a hatch. Although now modernised it retains that intimate and friendly atmosphere with 'children welcome everywhere if well-behaved'. There are all the traditional pub dishes but the 'specials' such as boeuf bourguignon and vegetable samosas really are special. Youngsters can have half portions. The Castle Inn on Edge Hill has many mementoes of the Civil War to add much interest to the visit and there is a magnificent garden with fine views. The pub has a comprehensive menu with a popular cold huntsman pie (a delicious mélange of chicken, pork and ham) and vegetarian options.

Miller; he invited many distinguished personalities to his social gatherings and Fielding is said to have written part of *Tom Jones* here. In the middle of the 17th century it was the family home of the American Washingtons and many years later Field Marshal Haig lived in the great house.

Horses have always had a role to play in this area. Once they were working animals in this rich agricultural region, which had its local blacksmith, wheelwright and carrier; today horse riding is popular and there are riding schools and stables in the village.

The route of the walk starts with a steep climb up Edge Hill. Slowly, with each step, the width of the lovely view over the Vale of the Red Horse increases (the horse was cut into the turf in Saxon times on hillsides above the village of Tysoe but it was ploughed up about 1800). We walk through the village of Ratley – a rather uncomplimentary name for a pretty

village with a late 11th-century pub – and on past another historic hostelry, the Castle Inn, perched on top of a wooded escarpment. There is a tower modelled by Sanderson Miller on Warwick Castle's Guy's Tower. It was sited to mark the spot where King Charles raised his rallying colours before the great battle of Edgehill. The return is through hill pastures where there is a magnificent view over a chequered countryside, then by a pond where ducks play and by the Grange and church.

THE WALK

❶ From the road junction in the centre of Radway walk along the lane away from the church. A step or two past the junction take a signed path up a vehicle track on the right. Walk to the end. Go through a kissing-gate where there is an ancient seat to rest awhile.

❷ Maintain the heading to climb a double step stile. There is now a steady climb through a pasture along a well-

PLACES of INTEREST

Upton House (National Trust) is 2 miles south of Radway. The place dates from the 17th century and contains a fine collection of paintings from various European schools. There are also delightful gardens containing a classical mock temple by Sanderson Miller. Upton is open daily from April to the end of September. **Shenington airfield** is a disused RAF base 5 miles south of Radway. There is a plaque at the entrance; it was at Shenington that much of the experimental work on the first practicable jet aircraft was undertaken. In the Castle Inn bar there is a finely drawn print by the noted aviation artist Ken Aitkin of the E28/39 Whittle aircraft.

The picturesque old post office at Ratley.

walked path to a kissing-gate and into woods. Turn left. At once the path divides; take the right-hand way to climb steps – take your time as there are 53, then another 36 to a road.

❸ Cross to the opposite road which leads to Ratley. Keep ahead at a meeting of roads to drop down High Street then Church Street to reach the inn. The Rose and Crown was originally built as a cottage for the stonemasons building the church and there are reliable (?) reports of a friendly Roundhead ghost here. Retrace your steps, passing the church, which has an unusual dedication – to St Peter ad Vincula – and the 'First Post Office' (in

use from 1882 to 1932). As the road twists sharp right keep ahead to pass a silver birch tree.

❹ By the gate of Manor Farm climb a stone stile. Follow the arrowed direction to walk by the right-hand border of a pasture a few steps then drop down the steep hill to a stile by a metal gate. Go up a hill to the diagonal corner of a field. Climb a stile by a corrugated iron shelter.

❺ Turn right to walk alongside a right-hand hedge. Go by a plantation of saplings (on a filled-in quarry) to a lane. Turn right then left after 50 yards. The fenced path leads to a road. Go left then right by the

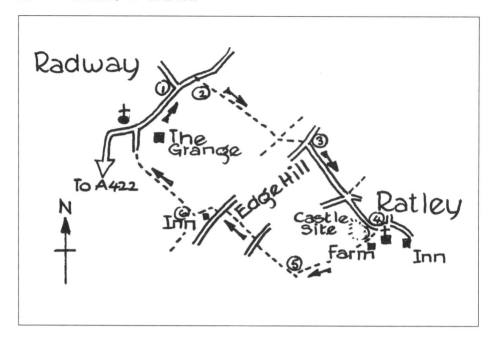

Castle Inn. The path descends to a meeting of paths.

❻ Go over the nearby stile (there is a stone seat here). Descend the ridge along a well-walked path, with Radway Grange in the valley away to the right. Go through a corner gap and continue over a stile and through a kissing-gate. Walk along a vehicle way to a lane which leads to a road. Turn right to the village centre.

ILMINGTON

Length: 7 miles

Getting there: 4 miles from Stratford-upon-Avon on the A3400 turn southwards along the lane to Ilmington.	Parking: There is a car park at the playing field in Mickleton Road.	Map: OS Landranger – Stratford-upon-Avon (151). (GR 210440).

Ilmington is said to be the most attractive village in Warwickshire. It is a delicious amalgam of brick and limestone buildings, the stone having been quarried over the centuries from the hills above the village. (The quarries have long ceased to be worked and the grassy area is now called the Humpty-Dumpty field!)

The name of Ilmington comes from 'elm-grown hill' but those lofty, billowing trees which once lined all the lanes have long since suffered from the ravages of Dutch elm disease. Overlooking the houses is the tower of St Mary the Virgin church. The Normans have left many marks in the church but the modern furniture by Thompson of York is also a fine feature. Children love to seek out the eleven mice carved by the manufacturer.

There is much of interest here, including an Elizabethan Manor House (with the pools where fish were 'stored' before the era of refrigerators!), an animal pound opposite the village hall (which was part funded by the Carnegie Trust in 1933) and the Catholic church in the old school building on the Upper Green. The delightfully-named Grump Street has one of the oldest houses, called Crab Mill – the crabs were of course not the marine variety but wild apples.

Ilmington still has its Morris dancers – this group is in fact the sole traditional one in Warwickshire, with a history going back 300 years. Some rather cruelly aver that it looks as though some of the participants are 'originals'!

The walk starts at the playing field car park. The wonderful sports area here was the result of one of the very first lottery fundings. Across pastures the paths rise to a pool which was to have been the focus of a spa as the waters were said to have healing properties when they were discovered in 1684. Tranquil paths now cross upland sheep pastures with far views over Meon Hill and its crowning hill fort; above us is the highest point in the county. The return is over Ilmington Down with a fine view of Foxcote – an 18th-century Palladian mansion – and through the lovely village centre.

THE WALK

❶ From the car park on the playing field walk directly across the field (with the pavilion on the left) to a kissing-gate which is to the right of far swings. Maintain the direction over the pastures to pass through a gate by the new school, attractively built in local stone. Turn right along a fenced way. Turn a left corner to a stile into a meadow.

❷ Regain the old heading to cross to another stile. The waymarked route now keeps ahead. At the end of the third field

THE ILMINGTON POUND
THE SITE OF AN ENCLOSURE WHERE STRAY ANIMALS
WERE KEPT UNTIL THEIR OWNERS HAD PAID A FINE
ITS USE GRADUALLY DECLINED AFTER THE
ENCLOSURE OF THE COMMON FIELDS IN 1781

The village pound at Ilmington.

climb a stile and bear left then right to resume the old heading. The chalybeate spring is nearby.

❸ The path climbs a gentle hill. After 200 yards you reach the little summit and a stile to climb on the left. At once climb another. Here is a wonderful 'welcome' sign. The owner has with the co-operation of the Countryside Commission created a long-term 'permissive' path.

❹ Follow the waymarks to keep at the left-hand side of the field. Do not climb the corner stile but turn right alongside a left-hand wire fence. The path drops downhill and goes left through a corner fence gap. Past a spring, join the right-hand border of the field and climb the hill to a bold bridleway.

❺ Turn right. Do not go right to barns but keep ahead to a large hill pasture. Bear slightly right. On the crest of the ridge look for a stile and little bridge over a stream. Over the water continue a few steps to a gate. Cross a brook. Bear left up the bank.

❻ In a rough pasture walk near the right-hand edge (a house is just seen to the right) to a way into woods. Follow the

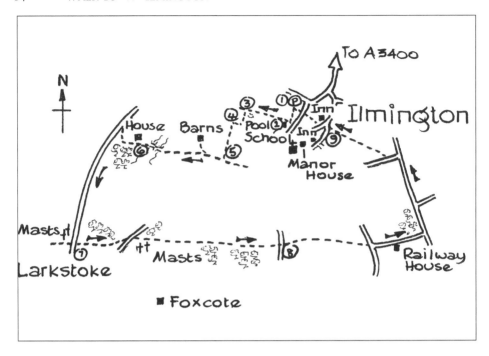

arrowed (sometimes muddy) path which soon swings right to a usually arable field. Take the signed direction over the field to a lane, an old drovers' road. Turn left.

❼ At TV masts (the highest point in Warwickshire) turn left. The unsigned bridleway runs alongside the remnants of an old low stone wall. In a far corner go through a bridlegate to a pasture. Go past a large oak tree to a gate to a lane. Cross to the farm 'road' almost opposite. Pass radio masts and follow the farm way (with a wonderful view of Foxcote) to a lane.

❽ Cross to the signed bridleway opposite. Follow the way of horses to pass through gates and drop down to a junction of lanes. Cross to the opposite lane and follow it past the old railway house to a T-junction. Turn left then left again after ½ mile. Within 200 yards take a signed path (Centenary Way) on the right. Follow the arrowed direction over the brow to pick up a right-hand hedge to a far corner and continue to a road at Ilmington.

❾ Cross the green. Just past the entrance to the Howard Arms car park and a house drive take an unsigned path between houses. Follow the path to a lane. Cross to the opposite path to pick up the early outward path. Retrace your steps to the car park.

TYSOE

Length: 5½ miles

Getting there: 10 miles south-east of Stratford-upon-Avon along the A422 take the signed lane, southwards, to Tysoe.	Parking: In Main Street or perhaps on the lane by the church.	Map: OS Landranger – Stratford-upon-Avon (151). (GR 341444).

There are three Tysoes – Lower, Middle and Upper, although many centuries ago the little hamlet of Lower Tysoe was Temple Tysoe as the manor was owned by the Knights Templars of Temple Balsall. The village is in what is known as the Vale of the Red Horse. The horse, cut into the turf over the red soil by the Saxons, was the horse god Tui which gave the village

its name. It was obliterated by ploughing about 200 years ago.

Tysoe (given by William the Conqueror to one of his followers, Robert de Stafford, in recognition of his support in battle) was once of great importance in the county – little smaller than Warwick itself. Nowadays, alongside the new estates, there are still plenty of old build-

FOOD and DRINK

The pub in Middle Tysoe is the Peacock with a fine sign and baskets tumbling with pretty flowers in summertime (although some say that it served as a mortuary for the fallen at Edgehill in 1642!). There is a wide range of good food on the menu but have a look at the 'specials' board if fish is your favourite dish. Game in season is also served, as well as the popular 'with chips' meals. There is a shop in Main Street which stocks fare for a picnic – and a good selection of ice cream for after the walk!

ings constructed with the local ruddy brown/cream-hued limestone.

The church dates from Norman times although there were many additions in the following centuries. There is an attractive octagonal Perpendicular font depicting many figures, as well as ancient brasses and window glass.

On the walk we have many views of what, 'lying like a dream in a hollow', is said to be the 'most perfect picture-book house of the early Tudor decades.' It is thought that villagers were expelled in the early 16th century when Sir William Compton built the great house in brick around an earlier structure. It is now the seat of the Marquis of Northampton but unfortunately the historic treasures cannot be seen by the general public.

The walk starts by the church and we pass several Biblical references to water, carved in stone by pious Victorians, before taking the field path to a hilltop windmill, beautifully restored. The route passes the elegant gates to Compton Wynyates then is along narrow, typically English lanes. In a field is the Compton Pike, a stone beacon assigned to the late 16th century.

The last leg of the walk is over fields.

THE WALK

❶ Enter the churchyard and walk along the path, keeping the church on your right. Leave the churchyard through wrought iron gates and continue along Saddledon Street, so named because just before the start of the Civil War at Edgehill in 1642 the Royalists resaddled their horses here after a hurried meal. By the inn turn right along Main Street to pass shops.

❷ By the war memorial is a road junction. Take the way to the right (Sandpits Road) which is signed to Oxhill. At a T-junction turn right (signed 'Oxhill') then at once left along Windmill Way. Keep along the estate road and maintain the heading along a short path at the end to continue along another estate road to a T-junction.

❸ Turn right. Within a few steps turn left down Smarts Lane. At the end go over a stile. Keep ahead a few steps then by a fenced waterworks turn right over the ridge and furrow pasture.

❹ Climb a stile to an often arable field. Turn left to walk alongside a left-hand hedge. Go into the next field and continue by a left-hand hedge, steadily climbing the hill. Go through a far corner gap. In a meadow walk to the left of the windmill to climb a stile.

❺ At once turn right to go through a little wood. In a corner turn 90 degrees left. Drop down the hill alongside the

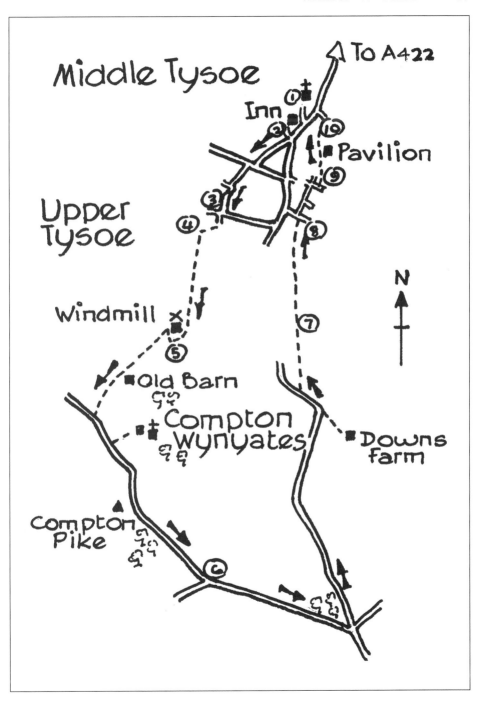

The windmill at Compton Wynyates.

PLACES of INTEREST

Brailes church is along lanes 4 miles south of Tysoe. It is a beautiful church (called the Cathedral of the Feldon and with a 120 ft high tower) which was built from the profits of wool in the 14th century. Also at Brailes is Castle Hill – a lofty mound on which a motte and bailey fort was perched.

fence. Go over a corner fence stile and stay on the same direction. Walk to the right of a ruined barn to join a farm tractor way to a lane. Turn left to pass the gates to Compton Wynyates (with rather forbidding notices affixed).

6 Go past a road junction. At the next turn left (signed 'Tysoe'). Within 1½ miles pass the drive of Downs Farm. Some 200 yards further along the lane take an unsigned path on the right. Go over a plank bridge and wire fence. Take a direction 75 yards from (and parallel to) the left-hand hedge and lane.

7 Go over a stile under an isolated tree. Maintain the direction across the next field. Go over a stile by a hidden brook. Bear slightly right to pick up the line of a left-hand hedge and old barn. Climb a corner stile. Keep the direction (mind the nettles!) at the side of a field and allotments to a lane. Turn left.

8 Immediately turn right (Middleton Close). Keep ahead at a junction to reach a T-junction. Turn right. Within a few yards take a path, left, to go at the rear of garages.

9 Enter a playing field. Walk alongside left-hand gardens then climb a fence stile to the left of a pavilion. Keep the heading alongside a left-hand hedge to climb a corner stile by a wired gate. Regain the old heading now by a right-hand fence to go over a corner plank bridge and stile.

10 Cross directly over a pasture to a metal gate tucked in a far corner. Turn left through the gate. Within a few steps take a fenced path through a kissing-gate. This goes to Peacock Lane which leads back to the church.

LOWER BRAILES

Length: 5 miles

Getting there: Lower Brailes is 3½ miles eastwards from Shipston-on-Stour along the B4035.	**Parking:** Off the main road near church.	**Map:** OS Landranger – Stratford-upon-Avon (151). (GR 315393).

The church of St George is a magnificent building which has been called the Cathedral of the Feldon (the rich agricultural land at the south of the county as opposed to the wooded Arden to the north). It bears comparison to the 'wool churches' of the Cotswolds and indeed was founded as a result of the important wool trade.

In the prosperous medieval times this was said to be third-largest place in Warwickshire after Coventry and the county town. Today (with Upper Brailes) it has the air of a well-kept and well-loved large village. There are still several shops and a wealth of lovely houses and cottages – some of them capped by thatch. Here are beautiful gardens with many of those old-fashioned cottage flowers that are all but

WALK 20 ✳ LOWER BRAILES   91

FOOD and DRINK

The George Hotel (appropriately near the church featuring the same saint) has pleasant beamed bars and lovely gardens with curving pathways. In summertime the landlord is rightly proud of his hanging baskets. Meals here can be quite substantial but there are various lighter options, such as ploughman's lunches. The Gate Inn is just up the road at Upper Brailes. The bars here are small and cosy and it is nice to sit in a corner and hear the locals putting to rights all the troubles of Warwickshire (and the world). The bill of fare is modest but good value with an especially enjoyable homemade soup. There is one food store in the village, near the George Hotel.

forgotten, and roses cling to the walls and tickle the eaves.

Above all is the 120 ft high tower of the church. Inside the place of worship are many old treasures including an especially nice 14th-century decorated font.

The Roman Catholic church dedicated to St Peter and St Paul is charming, having been constructed in 1726 in the upper part of a 13th-century malthouse barn. There is a fine modern school but the building of the Victorian school with its little bell turret can still be seen. However, there is little left of the motte and bailey castle (at Upper Brailes) which guarded the Fosse Way – except the hill on which it stood.

The route starts along the main street and in the spring and summer you can admire some of those pretty gardens. Over fields the bottom of Brailes Hill is reached. The upland is the second highest point of the county and capped by the beech trees known locally as Brailes Clump (unfortunately no right-of-way footpath goes to the top). After passing an isolated farmstead

where there are wide views far over the vale to the Cotswolds the route drops down to the village of Sutton-under-Brailes, with another fine old church. The return leg is alongside a brook which runs through a golf course, constructed on (I was reliably informed) some of the finest farmland in the Feldon!

THE WALK

❶ From the church walk towards Shipston along the B4035. Within ¼ mile turn left down Sutton Lane. After 200 yards a footpath is signed over a stile on the right (opposite Jeffs Close).

❷ The path hugs the border of a field which you follow around to a stile. Take the waymarked direction to a lane. Cross to the opposite bridleway which goes past a white cottage and climbs through woodlands. The way can be muddy at times but climb the bank and continue along the drier way.

❸ Go through a metal gate to sheep pastures and walk alongside the right-hand fence. Pass a farm and keep ahead through

PLACES of INTEREST

The magnificent Elizabethan mansion of **Compton Wynyates** is 2 miles north-east of Lower Brailes. It is not open to the public but a fine view of it is possible from the nearby hilltop windmill. On a hill above **Long Compton**, six miles south, are the mysterious **Rollright Stones**. Much folklore is told about these boulders. The isolated King's Stone is said to be a king turned into stone by a witch. Nearby are the clusters of rocks which are the Whispering Knights and the Stone Circle.

Brailes Hill.

a gap to follow a tractor way alongside a left-hand hedge.

❹ By fir trees go through a metal gate. Turn left by the left-hand hedge of a meadow. Go through a corner metal gate and continue descending, now by right-hand wire fences. Go through a gate by woodlands and walk along a farm road.

❺ Within 300 yards climb a well-signed left-hand stile to an often sown field. Go over the open field to a far stile into an orchard. Maintain the heading to a stile tucked in a corner by the church. Continue to a lane and turn left.

❻ Go past the village green of Sutton-under-Brailes whose Manor House received national notoriety not so long ago. Here lived a wealthy recluse who took great pains to cover up her humble roots – following her death her history was discovered after much investigation on television. At once turn right along a lane signed to Stourton. Cross a brook then at a junction take a lane, left, signed to Sibford. After 300 yards climb a stile, left, to a pasture. Walk the length to a stile at the very far end.

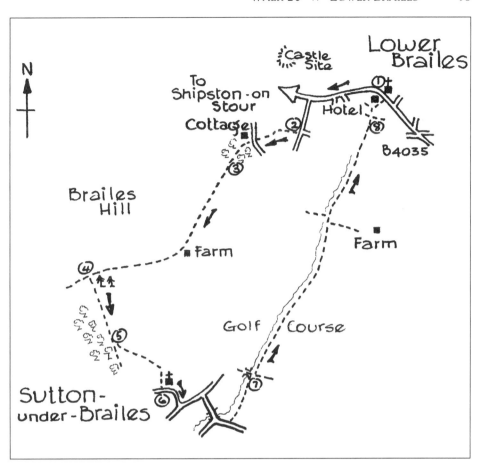

❼ On a farm track (a bridleway) turn right for a few steps then left over a double step stile to a golf course. The right-of-way path now hugs the bank of a left-hand brook. Continue through fields (crossing a farm drive on the way) with stiles showing the way – always near the brook.

❽ Nearing Brailes church we go through a field of ancient ridge and furrow farming. Cross a vehicle drive (two stiles) then follow the well-worn path. At a junction by a wall take the right-hand fork to Lower Brailes.